Teaching Citizenship

A companion website to accompany this book is available online at: http://education.leighton.continuumbooks.com

Please type in the URL above and receive your unique password for access to the book's online resources.

If you experience any problems accessing the resources, please contact Continuum at: info@continuumbooks.com

Also available from Continuum

100+ Ideas for Teaching Citizenship, Ian Davies
Citizenship Education in Japan, Norio Ikeno
The Citizenship Teacher's Handbook, Kate Brown and
  Stephen Fairbrass
Essays on Citizenship, Sir Bernard Crick
Rethinking Citizenship Education, Tristan McCowan

Teaching Citizenship Education

A Radical Approach

Ralph Leighton

continuum

Continuum International Publishing Group

The Tower Building	80 Maiden Lane, Suite 704
11 York Road	New York
London SE1 7NX	NY 10038

www.continuumbooks.com

British Library Cataloguing-in-Publication Data
A catalogue record for this book is available from the British Library.

ISBN: 978-1-4411-6510-7 (paperback)
       978-1-4411-0469-4 (hardcover)

Library of Congress Cataloging-in-Publication Data
Leighton, Ralph.
  Teaching citizenship education : a radical approach / Ralph Leighton.
     p. cm.
  Includes bibliographical references and index.
  ISBN 978-1-4411-0469-4 (hardback) – ISBN 978-1-4411-6510-7 (pbk.)
  1. Citizenship—Study and teaching. 2. Nation-building.
  3. Group identity. I. Title.

LC1091.L35 2011
323.6071–dc23

                                                          2011016518

Typeset by Newgen Imaging Systems Pvt Ltd, Chennai, India
Printed and bound in India

To my parents, with love and admiration

Contents

Acknowledgements

Many colleagues at Canterbury Christ Church University have engaged with the ideas and arguments put forward here – not always in agreement, but consistently with critical awareness, intellectual rigour and generosity of spirit. The most significant of these is Andrew Peterson, who is an inspirational and supportive colleague as well as a good friend. I have also been encouraged by Lynn Revell, John Moss, William Stow, Yvonne Stewart, and Trisha Driscoll, and by past and present members of the PGCE 11–18 team, all of whom I thank for their valued support.

The Citizenship Education community in the UK is wonderfully supportive, none more so in early stages of this book than Stephen Fairbrass and Lee Jerome. Richard Bailey, James Arthur, Ian Davis and Liam Gearon have also encouraged my attempts to grapple with citizenship education, and have been unstinting in their willingness to critically engage with my ideas – always to my benefit.

Any teacher worthy of the title learns from those they teach. Without the mixture of wonder, cynicism, enthusiasm, belligerence, insight, application, cussedness, patience, challenge, humour, questioning, inspiration and general teen-agedness of those I have taught in schools, this book would not exist. More recently, PGCE Citizenship students at Canterbury Christ Church University have kept me on my toes and sustained my confidence in the coming generations of teachers.

The invaluable contributions of Charlotte McGregor at WEDG, Linsey Cameron of the University of Kent and of my former students Durotimi Adeboye, Kola Adesina, Helen Loader and Philip Tutin are gratefully acknowledged and appreciated. My thanks also go to head teachers Liz Mahindru at Merrylee Primary School and Sarah Parker at Denbigh School, and to Tony Gilland from Debating Matters and Sophie O'Connor for their cooperation, and to Libby Tudball of Monash University, Australia, for alerting me to the programmes discussed in Case Study 8.

I am grateful for the support, advice and understanding of Ally Baker and everyone at Continuum who saw the glimmer of an idea develop into a book of which I am proud, and I hope they are as well. Ally's commitment to the project from the outset and her advice during its gestation and development have been key to its successful completion.

Most of all, appreciation and love beyond words go to Jo Letchford and our daughter Jen Leighton for their unstinting encouragement, patience and support.

Introduction

Preamble

In educational terms, the twenty-first century began in England with the establishment of citizenship education as a statutory subject for Key Stage 3 and Key Stage 4 which, it was claimed, would bring about a change in the political culture of the nation (Advisory Group on Citizenship 1998). Given how remarkably similar the 1990 National Curriculum had been to the requirements of The School Board Act of 1904, as explained by Bailey (1996), the introduction of a new subject might at least have been expected to bring about a change in the culture of schools. Yet citizenship education is in danger of becoming just like all other subjects by being constrained by the straightjacket of previous methods, previous expectations and previous outcomes – what Rudduck describes as 'innovation without change' (1991, p. 26).

Radical approaches

This book adopts some of the insights and arguments provided by advocates of radical and democratic approaches to education to demonstrate that citizenship education can become a liberating and empowering force for change. It is less about 'how to' or 'what to' and much more about 'why to', a book intended to encourage readers to think about the nature of the subject and about the experiences of those who study it and those who teach it. As Blake et al. observe, '[e]ducation is not the determination of who the student should be, but of how she might become' (2000, p. 195), not a process for inducting pupils into a mould but a series of experiences which will enable them to fulfil their potential – this surely applies equally to teachers and pupils, that the journey and the process and the experience of our development *is* our education.

This introduction provides an overview of the book and the contexts for which it has been developed, including the increased expectations for Master's Level work for student teachers and for practising teachers – and how this can benefit their teaching rather than being one more hurdle or a means to promotion. A key principle throughout is the notion that '[e]ducation for Citizenship equips young people with the knowledge, skills and understanding to play an effective role in public life' (QCA 2007, p. 27 and again p. 41). That sentence and those which come immediately after it are a call for action rather than passivity, for involvement not apathy, for excitement to replace boredom, to speak out instead of remaining silent, to understand how things are and how they might be improved. These are not typical ambitions in most classrooms in England but they are at the forefront of a radical approach to teaching citizenship education.

It is unlikely that any teacher underestimates the importance of their calling, and it should be of great concern to us all if they did, for there is nothing more important than education. As Baldelli

(1971) puts it, 'education is the process whereby competent persons come into being' (p. 88); he stresses the essential component of the role of the teacher as 'integrity' in much the same way as Blake et al. (2000) identify 'devotion', Draper (2001) writes of 'joy' and 'excitement', and Day (2004) emphasizes 'passion'. Any education, and that must include any teaching, which is not served by integrity, developed with excitement, imbued with passion and pursued with devotion, is guilty of 'mental warping and discredit' (Baldelli 1971, p. 88). If it is true that education in general is about developing competent people, then it has to be the case that citizenship education is about developing people's competence in their roles as citizens and that they are supported towards that end with integrity and passion, with joy and excitement. In turn we should be aiming to encourage and enable the desire for learning among our pupils and our students.

Radical approaches to education are not new, even if what constitutes radical must vary with time and place. Godwin (1797) explained that study without the desire to learn and to develop is not a real activity but a mockery. This remains true over two centuries later, and particularly true of radical citizenship education – an approach aimed at developing the desire to learn, to share, to understand, to acknowledge but not to fear difference, to understand and enable change. Indeed, while this is particularly true of citizenship education, it must be the aspiration of all education in all subjects and in all age-phases. As Blake et al. (2000) coherently and crucially argue, education without risk might meet the aspirations of bureaucracy and standards agenda adherents, but it isn't really education at all. When discussing the competing roles of technologist and philosopher which teachers might try to balance, they observe that the '[t]ranquillised acceptance of the technological approach is the real danger zone, the threat of a kind of nihilism' (Blake et al. 2000, p. 13). They are not arguing that technique is an inherently bad thing, nor that teachers should not be technologically competent, but that they must not become technocrats; the machinery and processes of education are simply tools to enable learning, and the question 'what is learning?' must matter more than the question 'can you see this at the back?' This is part of the radical approach to citizenship education, the approach which encourages thought and action – and a conscious connection between these – above process and passivity, which will enable both the subject and society to develop.

Citizenship education is not always taught with confidence or imagination, although that situation is reportedly improving year on year (Ofsted 2006, 2010). The introduction of Key Stage levels, public examinations, cross-curricular provision, and the recruitment of non-specialist teachers and non-specialist inspectors strongly implies that citizenship education is far from becoming 'more than just a subject' as proposed by the Crick Report (Advisory Group on Citizenship 1998). This book responds to the needs and aspirations of those who are dedicated to the ideals and principles of citizenship education but lack the time or opportunity – or lack awareness that they are not alone in aspiring to enable their pupils to make a difference – to clarify how best these can be achieved. Student teachers of citizenship education currently have a few supporting texts which are largely concerned with meeting school and National Curriculum requirements and expectations rather than offering an alternative and critical approach. Recent literature (Faulks 2006a, 2006b; Gillborn 2006; Leighton 2006; Clemintshaw 2008; Harber 2009; Brown and Fairbrass 2009) has identified a growing (re)awareness of the need for questioning and radical approaches to education in general and, for some, to citizenship education in particular. Within that discussion there is emerging an awareness that to plan lessons which address the National Curriculum concepts, processes, range and content and identified curriculum opportunities one by one or, even worse, to simply recycle lesson plans year on year, is to do a disservice to pupils and to society.

Context

While often identified as a subject arising from the findings and recommendations of the Crick Report (Advisory Group on Citizenship 1998), there has been provision for citizenship education as a cross-curricular theme since the National Curriculum was established in England in 1988. The introduction of the National Curriculum and other contemporaneous reforms of education were seen in many schools and by many teachers as a threat and a challenge, with specific allocations of time for some subjects, an official hierarchy of subjects, directions and directives regarding content and styles of delivery, cross-curricular themes, the establishment of a new system and style of inspections. New tests were introduced throughout primary and secondary education, and public examinations were reformed. It is no great surprise that citizenship education was largely ignored during such an upheaval, and there seems to have been no great sense of urgency on the part of government to enforce its own directives with regard to the provision of this particular cross-curricular theme.

The change in government from Conservative to Labour in 1997 heralded many reforms across political and social arenas, one of which was the eventual introduction of citizenship education as a statutory requirement at Key Stages 3 and 4. While Crick and his colleagues recommended that it should be introduced in 2000, the government delayed this in the expectation that schools would use the time to prepare. It is open to question how many schools took appropriate advantage of this time allowance, but one essential preparation not embarked upon early enough was the development of specialist teachers of citizenship education; this did not start at all until 2001 and not extensively until 2002, the year the subject was to be introduced into school, thus ensuring that this new subject began with a number of disadvantages which have yet to be fully overcome. Even now, a decade later, the number of places on pre-service programmes for teachers of citizenship education has been limited to the extent that there are not enough specialist teachers to ensure that every school in England has at least one member of staff who has studied citizenship education as their specialism.

An inevitable consequence was that teachers were under-prepared to develop and deliver what has been referred to as a 'soft-touch' curriculum. After 14 years of teaching to the National Curriculum and therefore being told what to teach, and sometimes how to teach it, those same teachers were suddenly expected to work out how to be creative and innovative, producing learning activities which would emphasize the nature of citizenship 'as more than just a subject' (Brett 2004) in a field of learning which was neither their specialism nor often of particular interest to them. Textbooks were produced and purchased before anyone had a clear sense of what was to be taught, never mind discussing who was going to teach it. By the time some thought appeared to have been given to the more crucial issue of what should be learnt – not always the same as what should be taught – schools had already planned either their delivery of citizenship education or their strategies to avoid delivering it (Leighton 2004c).

The situation therefore arose that student teachers of citizenship education were being supported in their development by people with varying degrees of expertise in teaching but virtually no experience of teaching citizenship. Even those teachers who, like me, qualified to teach before the National Curriculum was introduced, and had been involved in developing programmes of study which were aimed at raising awareness of social and political issues for several years prior to the Crick Report (Advisory Group on Citizenship 1998), could only claim limited experience of teaching the subject. Many school-based mentors had less experience as well as varying degrees of interest in the subject, so that the first few cohorts of specialist qualified teachers of citizenship education were supported by people still trying to work out how best teaching and learning might be achieved. This book represents the thinking behind some of my own attempts to work that out.

Purposes of this book

Where Sellar and Yeatman introduce their unique perspective on education with the observation 'that for every one person who wants to teach there are approximately 30 who don't want to learn – much' (1976, p. vii) they did not have citizenship education in mind. If they had, they might have added something to the effect that there is also a staffroom full of people who don't think it should be taught – much – and not by them.

One of the aims of this book is to eradicate that attitude. All teachers have to accept their responsibilities as teachers of citizenship education as well as of whatever other subject(s) they are qualified to teach. Poor awareness of chronology, speech patterns, scientific processes, arithmetic, courtesy, locations, aesthetics etc. by teachers of any subject could result in equally poor awareness amongst their pupils. The same is true of citizenship education, with even greater repercussions for society. All teachers are teachers of citizenship education.

Another aim is to encourage a more complete approach to education in general. Emphasis is often placed upon the accumulation of 'facts', of little snippets of information which are mistaken for learning and understanding, those things which can be easily identified, examined and measured, which constitute one part of what Harber (2009, p. 31) describes as lopsided education. It has been pointed out (Rattray Taylor 1974, Rudduck 1991) that apparently new terminology or new approaches to learning often transpire to be nothing more than cognitive education in a different format – as if wearing a new hat would make me a different person. Currently, even the National Curriculum emphasis on skills appears to require naming and explaining such skills rather than demonstrating and developing them. It is true that some employment-focused knowledge and skills are demanded by the National Curriculum – and, we must recognize, by pupils and by the adults responsible for them – but, '[s]uch skills are, of course, necessary. But in a human sense they are trivial' (Rattray Taylor 1974, p. 222). Our pupils will leave school and, in most cases, be in some form of employment for about 30 per cent of the day for about 85 per cent of the year for less than 75 per cent of their lifespan – or roughly 20 per cent of their post-school existence – but they will exist as people all the time, throughout their lives; we have to allow them the opportunity to develop more than skills for work.

Considerable progress is being made in the development of initial teacher training and in continued professional development for teachers of citizenship education. However, the emphasis largely continues to be on what to teach and how to teach it, rather than on why citizenship education should be taught and how best its objectives might be met. A subject in which questioning is fundamental appears to have been developed without questioning itself. Another of the key aims of this book, therefore, is to encourage teachers and student teachers to challenge that approach, to be more questioning of themselves, their peers, each other, and of the subject; the purpose of that questioning must be to gain a deeper understanding of what we are trying to achieve, and greater insights into achieving it.

This questioning approach must become integral to the work of teachers and student teachers of citizenship education. Not only in questioning why things are the way they are – or, even better, whether they are the way they seem to be – but holding all sources up to scrutiny and examination. On most routes to qualified teacher status (QTS) in England there is an option if not a requirement that student teachers begin to write at Master's level; ideally this will support teachers' development so that they also think and teach at (but not to) Master's level. This cannot be achieved without engaging in close scrutiny and critical examination of data, policies, arguments, practices and texts – including this one. Student assignments which cite one or two official reports (usually Crick and possibly one other) and a few chapters from one of the 'how to' textbooks, while often useful and informative, are not examples of Master's thinking and writing. The references in each chapter of this book indicate more closely the range of sources with which Master's students should engage.

To say that you agree with me because I'm right, or you disagree with me because I'm wrong, is not enough; these positions need to be explained, demonstrated, argued and supported with credible evidence. That is what Master's writing is about and what citizenship education should be about. There is a thoroughly understandable professional advancement rationale behind the pursuit of Master's qualifications, but an even more important motivation should be the enhancement of one's understanding of the skills and complexity of teaching, and therefore to be better equipped to teach.

Subversive education and radical approaches

The work of Postman and Weingartner (1976) shaped much of my understanding as a student teacher and my subsequent practise, and it shapes the approach taken in this book. I have borrowed from, applied and developed some of their ideas in order to demonstrate the need for belief, commitment and passion in citizenship education and that, even though they were writing at a different time and in a different place, and about the whole field of education rather than one specific aspect of it, their work remains relevant because so little of substance has changed.

The influences of a great many other writers, researchers and thinkers will be evident in this text. By no means all are educationists, nor are they necessarily academics or of a radical disposition; if citizenship education is to have any chance of success, it must be truly inclusive. Most of these writers have argued in favour of a questioning approach to life in general; not simply asking questions, but considering which questions to ask, and of whom – much in the same way, I hope, as teachers of citizenship education encourage their pupils.

Postman and Weingartner (1976) wrote of the potential for teaching to be subversive, a principle which can be applied in particular to the teaching of citizenship education (Leighton 2006). In substituting 'radical' I aim to reclaim a respectable term from media and political abuse and misuse. It is not a call to armed insurrection and a bloodbath of all who disagree, but a challenge to face up to and attempt to resolve some of the problems of society, to undermine the attitudes which result in suffering and the processes which result in feelings of hopelessness and alienation. Postman and Weingartner listed some of the problems of their time, and while both order and magnitude might have changed, the basic concerns have not.

The quality of living in the world's richest societies has not improved; if anything has changed at all, it is that we can add further social ills to their 'litany of alarm' (Arthur 2003). Religious fundamentalism and religious intolerance have become problems which conceal and thrive upon other problems and which allow manipulation on all sides. Debt, once seen as the preserve of the poor, is now a personal issue which goes across social class as well as being a national problem on a global scale. There is the dichotomy of both falling standards and unrealistic expectations in a number of public spheres – and possibly in private as well. In the field of public involvement and representation we find a many faceted and interconnected set of problems: political apathy, political intolerance, political inertia, political disempowerment – and the problem of politicians who neither deserve nor earn respect. As Tenzin Gyatso, the fourteenth Dalai Lama, has observed,

we are in danger of losing touch with those aspects of human knowledge and understanding that aspire towards honesty and altruism . . .
No one can deny the unprecedented material benefits of science and
technology, but our basic human problems remain: we are still faced
with the same, if not more, suffering, fear, and tension. It is only logi-
cal to try and strike a balance between material development on the
one hand and the development of spiritual human values on the other.
(quoted by Lehman 1999, p. 166)

As people contemplate these potential, or inevitable, or imagined,
disasters, there is much metaphorical gnashing of teeth and rending
of garments – but hand-wringing is not one of the skills which citizenship education can or should be concerned to develop. It would
seem that many people think they can explain the world and feel
free to complain about the world; the point must be to change it.

Need for change

Over the years, many students have decorated their rooms or t-shirts
with the slogan 'we are the people our parents warned us about';
if any of my generation think this remains true, they are deluding
themselves. We are now the people our children warn us about. If
the current social order does not seek to address and resolve problems such as those mentioned above but instead, whether through
deliberate endeavour or casual oversight, allows them to continue
and to multiply, then that order must be scrutinized and exposed;
to do anything else is at best hypocritical and at worst it is damning
our children and their futures. The school pupils of today are, after
all, those who will inherit whatever the current generations leave
behind. One often hears of parents going to great lengths and making considerable sacrifices to provide for or protect their children;
ensuring that they live in an honest and principled society is one
way in which everyone's children can be protected.

The teaching of citizenship education should, at its best, equip
young people with the tools, knowledge, skills and information

through which such scrutiny can be conducted. The purpose and practice of citizenship education is not to produce mindless electoral fodder or obedient social drones overdosing on volunteerism and unconsidered beneficence, but to question a society which accommodates or even expects and accepts problems such as those mentioned above. With such a questioning approach, young people can be enabled to subvert values and structures shown to be bankrupt, while retaining those demonstrably effective and appropriate to their lives; it is crucial that they are supported and encouraged to identify moral bankruptcy and ethical vacuums, and to be equipped to do something about them. It is from this position that I argue that the best teaching of citizenship education is both a subversive and an empowering process.

The notion that we need to get under the skin of an idea and of a society in order to really understand either is found in Lukes (1974), and the approach I advocate in this book stems in part from his analysis of the nature of power. Just as those with power determine what we think about, so the National Curriculum determines what we teach about. Critical citizens need to be able to question everything, take nothing for granted, and to decide for themselves whether to accept or reject particular positions and analyses. To teach the National Curriculum for Citizenship in a critical and radical framework requires that we scrutinize what we are expected to teach about and that we enable our pupils to critically engage with their own learning. Not only do we need to understand particular topics, but such topics can only really be understood by critically considering the nature of the subject they comprise and by engaging with the bigger themes to which the parts contribute.

To offer one example: the Crick Report (Advisory Group on Citizenship 1998) centres on the teaching of democracy in schools. The National Curriculum for Citizenship requires that teachers demonstrate that democracy is the best, fairest, most effective, most just political system. Such a position can be put forward by a civics education approach which details and examines institutions of government but does not question them; this would be neither radical nor subversive. More importantly, it would not be effective. There are many forms of democracy and there are many flaws in democratic processes; to deny these truths to our pupils is to deliberately limit their understanding and to invite their scorn and incredulity. The result of such an approach will be – and has been – to either limit pupils' access to information or to distort their understanding of it. Much better, surely, to be honest with pupils by enabling them to scrutinize democratic and other political systems so that they can come to their own, well-informed conclusions.

To do this is to be radical, in terms of state-provided and -monitored schooling, in that citizenship education would have to embrace and reflect educational ideas and actions which are significantly different from current practices. More than anything, it requires trust in the classroom. Trust in our abilities as teachers to support pupils' learning, trust in our pupils' abilities to learn and to think independently, and trust in their teachers by the pupils. As Peters and Bulut paraphrase Willis, 'radical educators should see the resistant actions of youth . . . and engage with them' (2010, p. 27). Postman and Weingartner identified the efficacy and accuracy of pupils' crap detectors, and we forget about these at our peril.

Synthesizing utopianism and pragmatism

There is a possibility that the reader will, by this point, have dismissed my approach as idealistic, that 'it's all very well in an ideal world but this is utopian nonsense'. I have no objection to utopianism in education, finding it immeasurably preferable to dull pragmatism or unthinking ritualism, but the ideas and actions of a radical approach to citizenship education have to be rooted in reality; this is one reason for the case studies which feature in each chapter – to show what is being done beyond the mundane and predictable. These 'case studies' might be better described as a series of examples from either theory or practice which illustrate what can be achieved. They are not being held up as paragons of citizenship education, but as encouragement to teachers of citizenship education. They are grounded in reality and give us real examples to which we and our students – and our colleagues in school – can aspire.

The determination to keep things real is also why I have referenced the National Curriculum (QCA 2007) and Ofsted reports. We have to work with the National Curriculum – it indicates what is expected in the teaching and learning of citizenship education and, while it is certainly not beyond criticism or a need to be overhauled and scrutinized, it provides the basis of the subject. That does not mean it should be regarded as a teaching target or the limits of what can and should be achieved, but that it is a starting point. Similarly, Ofsted inspections do not represent the pinnacle of either endeavour or achievement, but their reports do give some indication of what is happening in schools and it would be folly to ignore them.

The chapters in this book represent what I consider to be some of the key issues and themes of citizenship education, and the content of some is based on previously published articles and contributions to other texts. All are informed by my experience of teaching citizenship education in school and of supporting the development of PGCE Citizenship Education students at Canterbury Christ Church University. I have consciously avoided a narrow focus on specific topics within the National Curriculum because the National Curriculum for Citizenship does not have to be taught topic by topic. The nature, purpose and challenges of the subject are much greater than that, and it is with challenges that we begin.

It is the nature of any textbook on citizenship education that it will become dated by the time it is published. With the intention of minimizing that effect on the content of this book, a website has been established at http://education.leighton.continuum-books.com which will be updated every six months for the next few years. In this site there is advice for tutors and student teachers, a list of websites which can offer further insights – both theoretical and practical, and there will be further case studies. It is not in the nature of a radical approach to tell other people what to do and how to do it, but there must be scope for sharing ideas and experiences. Kolb wrote that 'Learning is the process whereby knowledge is created through the transformation of experience' (1984, p.38), and it is intended that the website will enable all of us to continue to learn how to teach citizenship education. Just as we know that presenting pupils with opportunities to learn from their experiences will enable them to continue to develop as active and responsible (but hopefully not compliant) citizens, it will hopefully prevent us from becoming predictable, complacent and compliant teachers.

Summary

The teaching of citizenship education as a radical and subversive subject can and will change the world. Something has to.

Teaching Citizenship

Preamble

The stated aim of the secondary National Curriculum for England (QCA 2007) is to enable all young people to become successful learners, confident individuals and responsible citizens – not only through citizenship education but through all subjects. All teachers are enjoined to ensure that links are made between their subject 'and work in other subjects and areas of the curriculum' (QCA 2007, p. 48). To a significant extent, then, all secondary teachers are teachers of citizenship education just as they are teachers of mathematics (particularly but not only numeracy), English (particularly but not only literacy), ICT, and everything else which pupils experience through both the overt and the hidden curriculum. This is a considerable challenge, particularly as few secondary teachers have the experience or expertise to deliver across the curriculum, and even more particularly when their responsibilities now include a subject – citizenship education – of which many have little knowledge or experience, and some have little awareness or interest. Fortunately the National Curriculum identifies and explains what many of these subject links are, but it offers less on how they might be achieved. As Bernstein (2010) notes, however, our concern should not be about covering the curriculum but about uncovering it – not regarding it as something to be delivered but as something to be understood, engaged with, investigated, interrogated, interpreted and used as a tool to enable pupil learning and pupil development.

Below we examine some of the challenges faced by citizenship education teachers, particularly the diversity of types of citizenship teacher, their backgrounds, and their needs; and provide some strategies to support and develop them.

Background

There can be no doubt that whatever progress has been made since the subject was introduced in 2002, some schools are meeting the National Curriculum requirements for citizenship education to the letter rather than the spirit, and others are failing to go even that far (Ofsted 2003, 2006, 2010; Leighton 2004c; Gillborn 2006; Faulks 2006a; Kerr et al. 2007). There are schools where the senior staff are not at all clear about what the National Curriculum for Citizenship entails, never mind whether the school is adhering to it, yet many of those schools offer good citizenship features in pupil experiences of teaching and learning, and in extra-curricular programmes. Equally, of course, there are other schools where senior staff have the same low level of understanding, and it shows.

The big question in the late 1960s was '[w]here do we get the new teachers necessary to translate the new education into action?' (Postman and Weingartner 1976, p. 130); in England since the Crick Report (Advisory Group on Citizenship 1998) was presented, the question has been 'where do we get the teachers necessary to implement the National Curriculum for Citizenship?' While some of these pioneers have been drawn from the ranks of serving teachers qualified in other subjects, most have come from elsewhere and by no means all people teaching citizenship education are trained to do so. For many, it is nothing more than a headache and a timetable filler just as has been the case for Personal, Social, Health and Economic Education (PSHEE) in its various incarnations, for Religious Education and for many other subjects to a lesser extent. It has also long been the case, however, that when a teacher is required to teach outside their subject they rarely do it with as much commitment, confidence and capability as when they teach the subject for which they are trained; this is something which those who chose not to employ specialist teachers either do not know or do not care about, and neither excuse is defensible.

The shortage of specialist teachers of citizenship makes the strategy of filling in with people lacking expertise inevitable in the short term, but we have to wonder whether it really is a short-term strategy. To date there are little more than half the number of teachers qualified to teach citizenship education which are required to ensure that all state secondary schools in England have at least one specialist; that initial teacher education programmes in the subject are oversubscribed indicates there is no shortage of potential citizenship education teachers. The DfE-sponsored continued professional development course for serving teachers to train as subject leaders in citizenship education has under-recruited in each year it has run, suggesting that most teachers are not inclined to retrain outside their areas of interest, that some of those who are so inclined are not interested enough to give up the weekends required to follow the course, or that school managers are not interested enough in the subject or their teachers or their pupils to inform or encourage non-specialists with regard to such courses. This distinct shortage in dedicated, specialist teachers, with an understanding of the content and skills required of this compulsory subject, should result in competition between schools to ensure they can recruit such a specialist. As some schools have already recruited two and a few have three, and some specialist teachers have left the profession either temporarily or permanently, such competition should be intense. However, not only is there no sign of intense competition to recruit specialist teachers of citizenship, 'with few schools advertising to recruit a specialist citizenship teacher' (Clemintshaw 2008, p. 83), but many such specialists find themselves filling other teaching posts (Leighton 2004a) or being required to supplement their timetables with subjects outside their expertise, and the uncertainty of employment remains a real concern among postgraduate student teachers specializing in citizenship education.

Citizenship education teaching and learning

Citizenship education should be about being critical, learning that learning can be fun and that there are as many right answers as there are people searching for them. Many schools are now developing collapsed timetable days for the delivery of citizenship and other curriculum areas (see Case Study 3). At one such school, staff expressed considerable reservations regarding the programme planned by my citizenship education specialist student teachers; they thought the work was too advanced, too challenging and beyond the comprehension and competence of their pupils. By the end of the day, those same teachers expressed astonishment at the quality of work produced and the application demonstrated by pupils often perceived as problematic in class. Citizenship education teaching can therefore simultaneously challenge and support those teachers who settle for medium goals, for containment and control, rather than aiming to enable and encourage their pupils. It is to the credit of those teachers that they were quick to see and accept that their assumptions had been misplaced, and that they have continued to work to further develop strategies which challenge their pupils; but far from all teachers react like that. If they did, we would never have heard of the self-fulfilling prophecy.

Paradoxically, this liberating and enabling function of effective citizenship education teaching and learning could be one of the things which militate against its wider deployment in schools. While teachers of citizenship education will encourage movement and participation, 'authoritarians always flinch and stiffen when children even move out of their desks, and when children move faster they see them as potential rioters' (Berg 1972, p. 13). If citizenship education can unlock doors and tap into potential, pupils will expect other subjects to do the same. They won't settle for mediocrity and passivity, so that effective citizenship education teaching and learning upsets the dependency on old teaching notes and lesson plans. It subverts other subjects and other classrooms and learning spaces.

When the Advisory Group on Citizenship (1998), Arthur and Wright (2001), Brett (2004) and others have contended that Citizenship education is 'more than just a subject', they have argued that the development of social responsibility and moral character require schools and teachers to develop new methods, new content, new activities and new approaches to learning. Citizenship education must be relevant to the lives of pupils and to the lives of those around them if it is to have any long-lasting effect. It is not a subject to be taught by assumed experts to a receptive and passive audience – it is difficult to perceive of good practice in any subject in this way – but one which requires pupils to question themselves and those around them, to learn as much about their own potential as about their rights and responsibilities, to understand and to participate and to contribute. Where the subject, its content and its presentation are not seen as relevant, it simply does not work.

Citizenship teachers

Non-specialist teachers of any subject regularly either try to fit their own discipline-defined strategies to the new to them subject or, more effectively, they adopt and adapt ideas from experienced colleagues. Given the significant proportion of practising citizenship education teachers who are not specialists, it is no surprise that many will work closely with student teacher specialists in order to make their own delivery of citizenship education more relevant to their pupils. Those teaching students and practising teachers have indicated some commitment to citizenship education and to ensuring its relevance to pupils as well as adhering to the National Curriculum. However, previous research (Leighton 2002, 2004a, 2004b) indicates that not all teachers of citizenship education see the subject requirements and their professional obligations in the same light.

The delivery of citizenship education in schools in England can best be described as erratic. This is certainly not due to a lack of information about the subject, given the plethora of internet sites, texts, documents, articles, handbooks and involved NGOs which proliferate, although the inconsistencies between these and the poor quality of some of these materials might be contributory factors. At least as important as such inconsistencies and erratic quality is the extent of the commitment of school leaders – which is considered in Chapter 2 – and the demonstrable disparity of types of teacher of citizenship education.

Most secondary school teachers in England have a degree in their subject as well as a postgraduate qualification in that subject, but the vast majority of teachers of citizenship education have degrees in subjects other than that which they have been trained or timetabled to teach. An earlier study (Leighton 2004a) identified one training cohort of 23 students as including graduates in nine subjects, who had worked with 27 school-based mentors whose qualifications to teach covered nine different subjects; only in the case of one mentor was that subject citizenship education. Since then, the institution where that cohort was studying has supported the development of a further 200 student teachers of citizenship education, only three of whom have had a degree in that subject. Currently, just under 30 per cent of the mentors involved in supporting new student teachers are themselves specialist-qualified citizenship education teachers, most of whom gained their qualification at that same institution. It follows that student teachers of citizenship education continue largely to have degrees in other subjects and to be supported by teachers trained and experienced in other subjects. Neither situation is inherently bad, but they do illustrate that citizenship teacher education is significantly different to that in others subjects – in few other subjects, if any, would it be expected that the great majority of applicants are graduates in almost any other subject except that which they wish to teach, that almost none had experienced the subject as a pupil or as an undergraduate student, and that the majority of those supporting their development were likewise lacking in experience of the subject as a pupil or as a student.

That research was based on interviews with student teachers of citizenship education and their subject mentors, and scrutiny of learning journals which the students completed as part of the process of reflecting on their professional progress and development, data brought together and considered in a framework of Interpretative Phenomenological Analysis (IPA – see Smith and Osborn 2003). This led initially to the conclusion that there were six distinct 'types' of teacher of citizenship education, but a wider ranging sample, further data and greater depth of analysis have revealed two more. While the classifications below (developed from Leighton 2004a and 2004b) are significant, they might not comprise an exhaustive list; the central issue is that there are many types of teacher of citizenship education.

1. *Commitment*: The decision to study to teach citizenship education is based on a belief in the underlying principles and content of the citizenship curriculum. Their academic backgrounds cover a wide range of subjects, and many have demonstrated their own active citizenship through political activism, working

for one or more NGO, or involvement in voluntary activities with faith groups or support networks. There is a strong identification with a sense of mission, a desire to 'make a difference'.

2. *Conversion*: Experienced teachers who recognize the importance of citizenship education to the extent that they are more interested in how to enable their pupils to acquire the requisite knowledge and develop the appropriate skills than in teaching their original subject. Some of these teachers feel that they do not have the necessary skills and depth of knowledge to develop the subject adequately and actively seek the recruitment of specialist teachers with whom they could work. Many of the teachers who enrol on the DfS-funded CPD courses for the teaching of citizenship will be 'converts', but not all.

3. *Convenience*: Some of those who have trained or who are training as specialist teachers of citizenship see it as a route into teaching their degree subjects, with the added bonus of being able to offer a Key Stage 3 subject which other teachers might not be able (or want) to offer. With few initial teacher education programmes in the social sciences, some graduates in related subjects consider their chances of successful recruitment and subsequent employment to be greater on citizenship education programmes. It is certainly the case that many sociology or psychology graduates who have completed a PGCE in citizenship education still teach, but some teach their degree subject rather than their qualifying one. Although not something for which those teachers can be blamed, it leaves us with fewer practising expert teachers of citizenship education.

4. *Coexistence*: There are teachers trained in other subjects who believe that there is a need for citizenship education teaching, not at the expense of their main subject but possibly complementary to their schools' PSHEE programmes; they often also perceive a need to prepare young people for life after school in ways which other subjects were not equipped to address. They tend to express what has been described (Leighton 2004a) as a 'Not before time' perspective. These teachers, and student teachers training in other subjects, are keen to deliver discrete lessons in citizenship education and to ensure the explicit inclusion and identification of the citizenship education curriculum in their own subject-specialist teaching.

5. *Colonization*: Some teachers believe that they can deliver 'their version' of citizenship education, in line with Crick's (Advisory Group on Citizenship 1998) notion that programmes of citizenship education could be tailored to the requirements of their school and the local community. This belief is based on the assumption that such requirements are both identifiable and identified, whereas such identification is often heavily influenced by the desire to protect and develop a particular pet interest or area of responsibility. Programmes of study which emphasize first aid, sex education, job applications and road safety, laudable as they might be, do not reflect the National Curriculum for Citizenship.

6. *Compliance*: Teachers of citizenship education who lack an adequate number of classes timetabled in their 'own' subject. Often younger and uniformly less experienced than their colleagues, they tend to want to avoid upsetting anyone who might be called upon to write a reference, so they do what they can. That they are compliant rather than dedicated or committed does not necessarily result in poorer teaching but it does produce greater anxiety for them, which is unlikely to benefit their teaching or their pupils' learning. More senior teachers who do not want to teach citizenship education are in a position to ensure they were not called upon to do so or, if so timetabled, they can find that the lessons coincide with 'unavoidable' meetings. In the past this left the lesson to be taught by a free and compliant or coerced junior colleague, something which agreements to limit the amount of cover a teacher can do is slowly changing.

7. *Conflict*: Some teachers are actively opposed to the teaching of citizenship education – either by themselves or by anyone else. Some of this might derive from insecurity with the subject material and ways of developing it: citizenship education tends not to be a didactically delivered subject. Other reasons for adopting such an oppositional stance include ignorance of the National Curriculum and the personal allocation of a relatively low priority to it. There are some, however, who know and understand the National Curriculum for Citizenship, who recognize its purpose and understand its strategies, and whose opposition is based on exactly those things; they are against the use of education as an enabling device. While such opponents of citizenship education might say it is a form of social engineering, the same could be said of any type or content of education; after all, education shapes society either through change or through maintenance of the status quo.

8. *Cynicism*: Those teachers of citizenship education who demonstrate cynicism are, largely, not cynical about the subject but about its likely success. One trained specialist, formerly a subject leader for citizenship but who has now reverted to teaching her degree subject, expressed concern that there were signs of her 'becoming cynical about whether we can make any difference to anyone'. Teachers such as these perceive (or recognize) that the subject is a timetable filler, sometimes without the homework or examinations which give status to other subjects. There can also appear to be a lack of support from school leaders and from other colleagues, giving rise to a sense of isolation.

All of these 'types' of citizenship education teachers represent individuals who require and deserve support, encouragement and development. Those who feel confident need to have their strengths developed, their skills enhanced, their knowledge base extended. So do all those others who teach the subject, whether they do so as a matter of convenience, colonization, compliance, conflict or cynicism. This is not only their entitlement, but the entitlement of the children they teach – every one of whom deserves the best of their teachers just as their teachers should expect the best of them.

Those who are committed, converted or operate within a framework marked by coexistence need to be equipped to support the development of the subject and the contribution it makes to the life of a school. They need to be enabled to keep up to date with ideas and initiatives and to contribute their expertise and experiences to the benefit of others. Those school mentors and other teachers who fit the colonization, compliance and conflict categories also deserve opportunities for support and development, but of a different sort. Insecurities have to be addressed and issues clarified. Whether the issue is of misunderstanding the nature and content of citizenship education or of working under duress and insecurity, the outcome will be limited subject development and low pupil achievement. Compliance and, to some extent, conflict arise from workplace bullying and are clearly in opposition to the principles of citizenship education. Colonization and some aspects of conflict deprive pupils of their entitlement to a full education, for which bullying is a rather mild term. Just as schools have anti-bullying strategies and systems which support victims and re-engage perpetrators, teachers are entitled to the same support.

Griffiths is correct when she writes that the essence of all things educational is

> learning, criticality, an opening out; and all this in a way which is personal and interpersonal, and which fits learners for life in wider society. This is a process which allows learners – and teachers – to change and develop their self-identities in ways which may be risky, but not to the extent of serious damage. Thus, education is concerned with both individual and collective well-being. It is highly personal and individual, and also highly social, political and public.
>
> (Griffiths 1998, p. 66)

If teachers are going to be allowed to change, encouraged to change, to take risks, their educational well-being must be considered, for it is by supporting them that young learners will also be supported.

Case study 1

I have no intention of intimidating readers with a tale of the stellar development of some super-teacher of citizenship education, a Weberian 'ideal type' or a Nietzschean superman (of either or indeterminate sex). Nor will I offer a heart-warming story of a poor lost teacher who found professional and spiritual redemption in citizenship education; 'To Serve Them All My Days', 'Dead Poets' Society' – works of fiction. Flights of fancy can serve a purpose, but we need to keep this real.

In order for teachers to begin to function as subversives, Postman and Weingartner (1976) suggest 16 principles of practice to be addressed. I adapted and developed them (Leighton 2006) to suggest some strategies for radical practice in the teaching of citizenship education, and have further refined my responses below:

1. *A moratorium on the use of textbooks* – the changing nature of what constitutes 'knowledge' in citizenship education, and the wealth of resources being produced by individuals, associations, NGOs and other agencies means that books are often used sparingly, to aid learning rather than as a substitute for learning. Subject specialists appear more willing (and perhaps also both more able and more confident) to do this, preferring to rely on their subject understanding to develop their own resources which can support their pupils' learning and development. For many schools, the low priority given to citizenship education means that there is little money for textbooks anyway, which can have benefits for the creative teacher.

2. *Teachers should teach outside their own specialism* – with so many citizenship education teachers originally specializing in other subjects and specialist student teachers largely being graduates in other disciplines, virtually all teachers of citizenship education are indeed teaching outside their specialism. Whether this is to anyone's advantage remains to be seen, but it should be beneficial to pupils if teachers can make links between subjects – just as the National Curriculum

Case study 1 *Continued*

requires them to do – and this is achieved more effectively when people teach outside their comfort zones, whether with regard to subject title or teaching strategies.

3. *Exchanges between primary and secondary teachers* – Opportunities for exchanges of information between primary and secondary teachers are not yet particularly frequent, although the increased federating of schools might create opportunities for more such exchanges. If citizenship education ever becomes a requirement within the primary curriculum, information exchanges and discussions should become more commonplace. Even without the statutory compulsion to bring citizenship education to Key Stages 1 and 2, many primary schools already demonstrate excellence in their approaches to Citizenship education (see Case Study 2) so there is no need to wait for someone to set up exchanges and discussion. When these do take place, they have to be on the basis that both phases have developed insights and experiences from which the other can benefit.

4. *Teachers who claim to 'know' their subject should write a book on it* – one of the consequences of the introduction of citizenship education was a plethora of books, not always written by teachers who could justify any claim to know the subject well. This has made the observation of principle 1. above all the easier to achieve and might equally apply to the overwhelming array of citizenship-education-related websites. Many teachers, not only those involved in citizenship education, already spend much of their time adapting textbooks, rewriting resources and developing their own; it is worth considering how their pupils might be involved in the process.

5. *Dissolve all subjects, courses, and especially course requirements* – this would require a seismic shift beyond the influence of citizenship education, indeed beyond the control of any state school, as it runs in opposition to the imposed National Curriculum. Many schools are ahead of the National Curriculum in their development of problem-based learning, integrated curricula, focus days and other approaches which emphasize commonality of subject content rather than the traditional separations. Citizenship education can lead the way with regard to course requirements – that every pupil is a potential citizen of somewhere should be enough. Leave grade expectation and entry grade requirements to others.

6. *Limit each teacher to three declarative sentences and 15 interrogatives per lesson* – citizenship education teachers need to be more interested in developing skills of articulate discussion among their pupils than in showing their own talents of oratory. It takes confidence in subject knowledge, a range of professional skills, classroom management which fosters involvement and learning rather than obedience and silence, and the belief in pupils' ability to engage for a teacher to step back from telling and asking, instead allowing pupils to ask and tell and discuss and challenge and learn. Limit the quantity of teacher talk without forsaking the quality.

7. *Ban teachers from asking questions where they already know the answer* – All teachers should strive to exercise such self-control. Clemintshaw (2008) points out that questioning is a vital technique in any teacher's armoury and, with care and forethought, teachers can use questioning strategies to great effect. Questioning is essential, but not those questions designed to show how much teachers think they know rather than those which develop pupils learning and understanding.

8. *A moratorium on tests and grades* – Many teachers resist pressure from pupils to offer grades while others see examination as a route to subject acceptance. The requirement to report on attainment and progress prevents any moratorium – which does not mean it is not worth considering, but that currently movement is in the opposite direction. If work must be assessed, teachers should consider formative feedback over summative grading; pupils will learn much more from reasoned advice than they ever will from a National Curriculum Level number written in a particular colour.

9. *Psychotherapy as part of in-service training* – perhaps even as an occupational entry requirement. It is certainly essential to have a strong support network – not sycophants, but people who will listen and understand. This might be why so many educators have partners who are also educators, because they can listen and understand; paradoxically, it might also account for the divorce rate between educators.

10. *Classify teachers by ability and make the lists public* – this is effectively one aspect of what league tables and, more explicitly, Ofsted inspections are doing. Criteria for 'ability' are contentious and contested, and this 'principle of practice' smacks of naming and shaming. Much more useful, and much more in the spirit of

Case study 1 *Continued*

citizenship, would be to have learning mentors where pupils talk with and work with teachers to identify what works well for their class and what does not. If this is non-judgemental – reflecting 8. above and not grading or assessing the teacher – everyone benefits.

11. *Pupils test teachers on what pupils know* – This happens daily in the citizenship education classroom, when pupils will offer examples and insights potentially alien to the teacher. Just as we remind our pupils, the teacher should remember that it's okay to get things wrong; indeed, it could sometimes be a really smart move which empowers pupils.

12. *Make every subject optional, with teachers paid only if their next option is taken* – it is becoming the case that some schools choose not to run courses which are undersubscribed, expecting teachers to then teach other subjects outside their specialism or move to other schools. The guiding principle in such cases is 'value for money' rather than quality of pupil engagement. This strategy would undoubtedly be both subversive and radical; whether it would be practical or helpful is more open to question. If, however, we planned and taught as if it were the case that our employment was dependent upon our pupils' engagement, we can be confident that teaching and learning would improve.

13. *One year off in every four for teachers to work outside education* – My anecdotal observation is that those students who come to teacher education with prior employment experiences, and who can recall them, do seem to have great tenacity and creativity in the classroom. The benefits are not all one way, either. Participants in Teach First, for example, agree to teach for two years before going into the industry or profession of their choice. While many find that teaching is much more rewarding than they expected and build careers in education, those who do develop careers in other fields take a range of skills and insights with them which benefit them, their colleagues and their employers. The greatest concern must be that teachers who experience the pay and conditions in other sectors might not return to teaching.

14. *Requirement of evidence that a teacher has had a loving relationship with at least one other human being* – the word 'other' is crucial here, as the teacher who puts personal preferences before

pupils' needs is not much of a teacher at all. While in no way belittling the love and support of my family, I have also found that sharing a house with a cat has helped me to keep my social worth in perspective.

15. *All graffiti from school toilets be reproduced on large paper and hung in school halls* – whereas the tendency is to use anti-graffiti paint. School desks remain a valuable source of information on student angst, and the growth in popularity of websites of pupils' views of schools is also instructive. A really effective citizenship education school, with its opportunities for pupil voices to be heard and identities and diversity to be celebrated, would not have graffiti anyway.

16. *Ban these words and phrases: teach, syllabus, IQ, make-up, test, disadvantaged, gifted, accelerated, enhancement, course, grade, score, human nature, dumb, university material, administrative necessity* – progress here has been uneven and not very impressive. 'IQ', 'dumb', 'human nature' and 'disadvantaged' have largely disappeared from formal educational discourse but can still be heard in staffrooms either explicitly or in barely disguised euphemisms. 'Enhancement' has a variety of synonyms dependent on context, often in relation to a student being 'gifted', which is in turn usually accompanied by 'and talented', without anyone being particularly clear about what they mean. Government attempts to blur any distinctions between academic and vocational experiences while aiming to enrol 50 per cent of school leavers into higher education with others entering further education renders 'university material' all but meaningless. 'Teach', 'syllabus', 'test', 'course', 'grade', 'score' and 'administrative necessity' clearly remain with us, with no signs of reduction in the near future.

To some extent these principles of practice could be regarded as an educational equivalent of the Charter for Parliamentary Reform which was promulgated several times in Britain in the mid-nineteenth century. At the time many of its demands were seen as far-fetched, outlandish and unworkable, but only one – annual Parliaments – has yet to be introduced. It may be that, in 170 years, Postman and Weingartner's list will be viewed as old hat; for now we should recognize that some of it is being achieved, most of it is achievable, and some aspects might have to remain aspirational.

Summary

Citizenship education teachers come from many backgrounds, offer many skills and have many differing needs. When citizenship education is allowed the freedom to develop most effectively and creatively, it can subvert the security and controlled environment within which so many teachers are cocooned and/or in which they cocoon themselves. This is both their greatest strength for their pupils and their greatest threat to their colleagues.

School Ethos

Preamble

It is important to note that the National Curriculum for Citizenship (QCA 2007, pp. 26–49) does not state what pupils should be taught, instead requiring that 'pupils should be able to . . .', 'the study of citizenship should include . . .', 'the curriculum should provide opportunities for pupils to . .'. The emphasis is not on teachers' ability to impart a body of knowledge; instead, pupils are expected to explore creative approaches, reflect on their own progress, debate, campaign, work in groups, have contact with NGOs and pressure groups. Crucially, pupils are also expected to have opportunities to be actively involved in the life of their schools, neighbourhoods and local communities which in turn presents 'opportunities for schools to address their statutory duty to promote community cohesion' (QCA 2007, p. 29). All of this requires planned movement away from traditional classroom activity, away from teacher-led learning, and away from the passive receiving of assumed (or confirmed) truths. Teachers and pupils need to know that the school not only supports and encourages such approaches to learning and development, but that it both insists upon them and provides an ambience within which these things take place as a matter of routine.

Blake et al. (2000) argue powerfully that, as educators, we should be concerned with the development of personal qualities, not simply of a body of knowledge and/or a range of skills.

> A caring person is generally caring (but) [t]o have caring skills or competences is rather different. . . . The skilful doctor, as Plato observed and recent grisly events in Greater Manchester have confirmed, makes an unusually skilful poisoner. But if you are a caring person . . . you will abhor the misuse of those skills through which your personality expresses itself. (Blake et al. 2000, pp. 17/18)

Similarly, a radical approach to teaching citizenship education is one which requires that pupils have opportunities through which to develop into socially constructive and involved citizens, people who not only know what is expected of citizens in relation to rights and responsibilities but who also see beyond statutory provision and the characteristics of good citizenship – to be aware, as Werder (2010) puts it, of their *response*-abilities, of how and why and to what extent citizens can and should respond.

This chapter considers how and why the day-to-day atmosphere, activities and relationships in a school indicate the true nature of that school, and how they are central to the status and development of citizenship education. It also looks at what schools can do to take citizenship education beyond the confines of classrooms to make it an integral aspect of how schools function and how people within them think and act. While it has been observed that citizenship education 'must involve the whole school and there must be a clear and reiterated rationale for the ideas of shared governance and distributed responsibility if participatory democracy is to prosper in the classroom and in the institution' (Reid et al. 2010,

p. 14), it does not always follow that those who run schools want democracy to prosper.

Background

It is almost 30 years since White and Brockington noted that a 'vast, untapped resource of human potential seems to pass through our schools unrecognised' (1983, p. 8), but it is fair to say that it remains true today that schools fail to make the most of what pupils bring with them. If citizenship education is to be successful this has to change. In Chapter 1 we touched upon some of the issues facing the effective development of citizenship education with regard to subject-specialist teachers, but by far both the biggest hurdle and the greatest opportunity is the ethos of a school and the extent to which this supports and advances the aims of citizenship education. Many schools will have a mission statement or endorsed policy or some such awkwardly designated eulogy to how wonderfully inclusive and developmental and holistic it strives to be, but what really matters is what the school does and what it enables to be done.

It is tempting to take a leaf out of the autobiography of former Arsenal, Bradford City, Newcastle United, Sunderland and England football player Len Shackleton – more accurately three leaves – when discussing the place of citizenship education in determining school ethos. According to Best and Scott (1994, p. 174), Shackleton's chapter on what club directors know about football consisted of three blank pages. The same would appear to be an equally fair representation of how much many head teachers and school-governing bodies know or care about citizenship education. I have resisted the temptation to go quite that far, settling instead for agreement with Ofsted where they observe that '[t]here remain schools where leaders have done little or nothing to respond to a National Curriculum requirement that has now been in place for seven years' (Ofsted 2010, p. 32). Some school management teams and governing bodies clearly consider that it does not particularly matter who teaches citizenship education, if it is to be taught at all. This belittles both the subject and the qualities of the staff involved, and it limits the opportunities for school pupils to understand and to make progress. It is also a position of both social disempowerment and rank hypocrisy.

When school leaders emphasize the importance of obedience to rules and authority they are in no position to then ignore the decisions of government, refuse to implement the National Curriculum and abrogate their legal obligations. When they claim to have school pupils' interests at heart, they should not then refuse to recruit expert teachers of citizenship education but instead require teachers whose expertise lies elsewhere to teach the subject to the detriment of all concerned. Those school leaders who proudly defend their autonomy on the grounds that the future of society is safe in their hands should not then prevent young people from being prepared for social involvement and social leadership. Such posturing is tantamount to saying 'citizenship education doesn't matter, you don't matter'. Pupils are citizens now, not some vague time in the future, and their roles, involvement and entitlement needs to be continually developed, as they do for us all. As Alderson observes in her critique of myths surrounding the place of citizenship education in schools, the notion that it is to prepare them as future citizens rather than current citizens is to regard 'school students as human becomings, and less than fully human beings. It is illogical . . .' (Alderson 2004, p. 33). It is hypocrisy of this sort which is symptomatic of the social reality citizenship education must seek to expose and subvert.

In the very early days of statutory citizenship education I was regularly told by experienced teachers who were supporting the development of my students that 'we don't do discussions in this school/department' and that 'the trainee needs to learn from me, not me from her/him'. Such narrow approaches to learning and to teacher development appear less frequently now, but were and are symptomatic of an authoritarian model of teaching and professional self-image which sits uneasily with citizenship education. That school management teams consulted with staff in only 29 per cent of those few schools where the subject had been introduced in the light of National Curriculum requirements in 2002 (Cleaver et al. 2003) does not bode well for the extent and outcomes of pupil consultations with regard to citizenship education in particular as well as with other aspects of their educational experience, and suggests that pupil voices (see Chapter 5) will have to be raised loud and long if they are to be heard. When established teachers expect specialist student teachers to work with non-specialist materials or wholly in ways conventional to and developed for other subjects, lessons are rarely as successful, nor are placements as successful, as when there is collaboration and innovation. Nonetheless such expectations are commonplace. It is also becoming clear that some schools welcome and develop a critical and questioning approach, inviting pupil contributions and striving to make sure that citizenship education is not only taught in innovative ways but that its content is and remains relevant.

It has been consistently shown (Leighton 2002, 2004a, 2004b; Ofsted 2006, 2010; Kerr et al. 2007) that schools approach the delivery of citizenship education in a number of ways, the effectiveness of which can vary enormously. Some schools integrate citizenship education into other subjects. This is often within one or more of the humanities, with RE featuring prominently, but also through English, or across the whole curriculum. In other schools it is conflated with PSHEE or sometimes subsumed into an existing programme, both circumstances often giving rise to acronyms which look like the product of a random letter generator (should such a thing exist), while in other cases a hybrid such as Personal and Citizenship Education (PACE) has emerged. There are many – a growing number – where citizenship education exists as a separate timetabled subject, others where it is presented through a series of collapsed timetable days or events, some which offer various combinations of these approaches and, regrettably, some where there remains no formal recognition or provision in fact even if there is in a policy document and aforementioned mission statement.

Even in those schools where there is distinct timetable provision of the subject, delivery is neither uniform nor consistent – not within each such school and certainly not across all such schools. There are schools, and there are teachers within schools, who follow the schemes of work and lesson plans available online made available by the Qualifications and Curriculum Development Agency and/or produced by commercial agencies, some following these to the letter while others use them to guide rather than dictate lessons. There are schools, and there are teachers within schools, who recognize the spirit of the National Curriculum for Citizenship and who have developed and present their own interpretation of it – and others who have developed and present their own version without necessarily paying close, or even scant, attention to either spirit or specified content. There are schools, and teachers within schools, who have relabelled lesson plans and re-jigged schemes of work which were originally intended for other subjects and other purposes so that they can pursue a pet theme irrespective of its relationship – if any – to the National Curriculum for Citizenship.

Although teachers of all subjects have been expected to contribute to pupils' entitlement to a citizenship education programme which is 'coherent . . . in terms of the concepts, values and dispositions, skills and aptitudes and knowledge and understanding to be acquired' (Advisory Group on Citizenship 1998, p. 35), not all are doing so, able to do so or being enabled so to do. The latest form of the National Curriculum requires that all teachers of all subjects ensure that their pupils are supported in identifying links with all the other subjects, but there is not yet conclusive evidence that this is happening on a wide scale. Even where it is happening, and ignoring the difficulties inherent in establishing such links if some subjects are either not taught by specialists or not taught at all, it is essential that the character of citizenship education is established throughout all aspects of the school – it must go beyond the classroom and into meeting rooms, social spaces, laboratories, study areas, sports and athletic arenas, publicity materials, websites, public presentations, dealings with suppliers, and the myriad other places and spaces which comprise the operations and sphere of influence of a school.

Citizenship education – a whole school imperative

It is not enough for pupils to be involved in citizenship education lessons once every week or so, if the rest of their school experience does not support and reinforce the value and values of the subject. Indeed, as Harber notes, 'the introduction of a subject aimed at democratic citizenship has merely highlighted gaps between the stated aims and practices of this area and the rest of what happens in schooling' (2009, pp. 89/90). We can predict with confidence that most schools in England expect the conventions of the English language to be observed in school communications, in assemblies, in taught subjects, on their website, by clerical and other administrative staff, and, where they are not, for the context and justification to be made clear or corrections to be made. It is equally predictable that schools will expect the laws of physics to apply in the day-to-day running of the school where appropriate, and would investigate a sudden loss of gravity or, a more likely event, disruption to the electricity supply. They will expect those with financial responsibilities, or with registration responsibilities, to be able to add and subtract in accordance with accepted arithmetic practice. IT systems will be expected to work, doors will be designed to open and close effectively, catering will be nutritious. In other words, the essence of most subjects pervade schools in their daily existence as one element of the hidden curriculum (Bowles and Gintis 1976). If citizenship education is not equally embedded in all aspects of a school and in all those who act on behalf of a school, it is not part of that school's ethos, irrespective of fine words and mission statements. If we want pupils to treat people with respect, they should be treated with respect; if we want pupils to participate, they must have opportunities to do so and be encouraged to make use of them; if we believe that pupil voice matters, we must listen.

Florio-Ruane offers us the wonderful term 'culturalectomy' (2001, p. 23) in her observation that schools often appear to conduct themselves on the assumption that issues of ethnicity, language and identity are irrelevant to teaching and learning, and she clearly demonstrates the fallacy and the potential costs of such an assumption. Schools, as with any other organization or social structure, are not value-free institutions; they either incorporate the cultures of the people who constitute the institution to synthesize a new, dynamic and inclusive culture, or they operate under an imposed and non-negotiable culture. As Florio-Ruane makes abundantly clear, schools tend to the latter model to the detriment of all people involved. Teachers and other staff members bring with them a range of cultural perceptions, as do pupils and student teachers. These perceptions will overlap with each other as well as with the overt culture of the school, and there will be times and places where the differences are as significant as the similarities. A school which ignores such diversity ignores the resource of human potential that it constitutes, a theme to which we will return in Chapters 3 and 4.

Schools should be celebrating that diversity of background, outlook and experience, and seeking to build upon it. Recognition of the rich variety of humanity which comprises a school can be achieved through lesson content in all subjects, through formal assemblies (whether religious, humanist or simply informative), through wall displays, extra-curricular activities, school trips, fund-raising events, social activities, website content, newsletters, publicity materials, school policies and practices, governors' meetings, and any and all other aspects of a school. If there are any exceptions – for example, if belonging to a faith is held to be superior to having no religious faith, or if one faith is held to be of greater truth or value over others, if there are no vegetarian options at social events, if parents and other carers feel excluded, if local communities are seen as irritants or irrelevant – then the ethos of the school is not a citizenship education ethos.

Acting in accordance with the old adage that actions speak louder than words, the next case study illustrates what one school has done to demonstrate the commitment to ensuring that pupils have the opportunity to become effective citizens. Of particular importance is that these things are not simply being done to meet legislative requirements, but because they are understood to be the right things to do.

Case study 2

Merrylee Primary School in Glasgow is a non-denominational co-educational primary school with 283 pupils aged between five and twelve on roll (in 2010), serving a socially and economically diverse area. After several years as a split site school, a new building was opened in 2009. The National Curriculum is not in place here because it applies 'to every British child's well-being (apart from those in Scotland and Northern Ireland and those attending independent schools – this is a National Curriculum in only a highly idiosyncratic sense of the term)' (Bailey 1996, p. 15). While there are the recommendations of the Scottish Curriculum to consider – according to the Scottish Government website, '[t]he curriculum is non-statutory in Scotland and so is not dictated by the Government. Responsibility for what is taught rests with local authorities and schools, taking into account national guidelines and advice' – as well as a school improvement plan to achieve and a number of National Priorities to be addressed, the impression given by this school is that these things are being done because they are the right things to do.

Case study 2 *Continued*

What is striking about Merrylee is that almost everything about the school is redolent of good citizenship education and active learning. What is presented in this case study is an example of what can and is being done to involve pupils, staff, parents and other carers, communities, the local economy and the regional polity in the life of the school as a matter of course. Some of the opportunities which the school has taken advantage of will not present themselves to everyone – just one example is the school's good fortune in both having a new build and simultaneously having an architect on the school parent body – but many more are the result either of careful and integrated planning or of the essence of citizenship education being the essence of the school. If it is the first then those involved are to be congratulated for planning for the future and with education as their focus; if it is the latter then so much more can be expected as and when needs and opportunities are identified. Whichever is the case, it is an example many other schools would do well to follow.

The new building has been designed in consultation with children, staff and parents. Built using materials which were lightweight and, where possible, from recycled sources (for example, newspaper serves as cavity wall insulation), it is oriented for maximum use of natural light and some walls are partly glass so that everyone can see the construction methods and materials and the insulation – ensuring a daily reminder of the importance of conservation. There is also a dedicated eco-classroom which looks out over the school's own wind turbine, itself partly financed by Scottish Power.

The school grounds also house the Urban Jungle. This is the first Natural Play site on any UK school campus, and is the outcome of discussions with pupils and consultation with the Forestry Commission, the school's own environment committee and its parent council and with Glasgow City Council. As well as making another contribution to environmental awareness, this is also an illustration of collaborative working, local democracy, working with a non-governmental organisation (NGO) and practical and effective parental involvement.

As well as having a pupil-elected school council in which every class has representation and which meets regularly with the head teacher, pupils at Merrylee have other opportunities in which to have their voices heard. Older pupils are consulted on some matters of curriculum development, while peer mediation and a buddy system allow a range of pupils to become involved in working with and supporting each other and to make representation to the school management team about issues which arise. Pupils also have the opportunity to be appointed to posts of responsibility which include referees, gardeners, litter patrol, ICT technicians, and librarians. In Chapter 4 we will go on to consider issues of identity – one of which is the notion that identity is about rights whereas it is character which is about obligations. If this is the case then Merrylee is clearly aware of the importance of character education.

The school offers many activities beyond the classroom and other designated learning spaces. It runs nine different sports clubs, including football for both girls and boys – an activity which is augmented by the school having its own, Scottish Football Association-approved pitch. There are ten other activity clubs including a pupils' allotment society, which was joint winner of the Millar Cup for Best Children's Allotment in Scotland. All such activities provide opportunities for healthy living, engagement with the local community, and for pupils to achieve a sense of fulfilment and achievement other than the academic. When pupils at the school were invited to test a new virtual reality game by the BBC and the University of Westminster, one outcome was that the teacher involved addressed an international conference on children in virtual worlds.

Even in the best run, most pupil-friendly, most inclusive and citizenship-focused schools, there will be times when someone's behaviour is seen as unacceptable. At Merrylee, the response to poor pupil behaviour is to try to engender a sense of responsibility for one's actions and the pupil makes amends by helping within the school community.

Many schools have PTAs and/or Friends' groups, generally seen by teachers as sources of fundraising for the school and providers of tea and cakes at open events, sports days and concerts. The approach at Merrylee is different.

The Parent Council has worked closely with the rest of the school community to go well beyond tea and cakes, pennies and pounds, while not neglecting these essential contributions to the school. By recommending a particular charity shop as the place to donate unwanted or outgrown items of school uniform, the Parent Council is simultaneously supporting the local community, a good cause and the principle of recycling. It is also a sensitive way to draw the attention of less well-off carers to a relatively inexpensive source for sought-after items. Their 'plant a tree scheme' not only contributes to improving the environment of the school, it is marketed as one way to offset carbon footprints and as a source of revenue for the school. A less obvious but none the less important contribution to the environment has been the Parent Council's preparation of information about safe parking and safe routes to school and their campaign for traffic-calming measures. These not only involve the local community but also contribute to a safer school. The Parent Council was awarded £1000 by the Millennium Commission, and used the money to fund a programme in which local children and older people worked together with artists and entertainers to produce a community show, thereby crossing age boundaries and enabling everyone to learn new skills.

Case study 2 *Continued*

We have not, of course, looked at the curriculum offered by the school, but we have looked at those aspects of the school over which those who run it have authority and autonomy. What we have seen is a community in which there is daily engagement with democratic processes through regular consultation, collaboration within and outside the school, with elected representatives and with NGOs. It is a school with environmental awareness at its heart, an awareness which is raised in many ways without scaremongering or shrill assertions, but where pupils can see and learn for themselves. School processes support the development of pupil character, offer a range of opportunities, reinforce gender equality and community involvement; pupils experience working with adults in a secure environment and on practical issues. All staff are also well supported in their development, with research involvement and conference presentation being a part of that. Parents and other carers are involved with, and on behalf of, the school.

When I left Merrylee Primary School in 1966 it had classrooms, a school hall, milk monitors, a playground and a red gravel football pitch, and recognition of pupils' non-academic achievements was the 'Citizen of the Future' prize voted for by pupils in their final year – I came second. I hope I have made some progress since then; the school most certainly has.

Summary

If those involved in running a school are not committed to the development of pupils as citizens, the subject will be no different to any other. School leaders, governors, administrative and other support staff, parents, pupils, visitors, the wider community – everyone has to be involved. Once they are fully involved and fully committed, opportunities to develop are limited only by the collective imagination.

Identity

Preamble

Identity and diversity are combined within the National Curriculum for Citizenship (QCA 2007) as one of the three key thematic areas of study; the others being democracy and justice, and rights and responsibilities. If pupils are to appreciate that all identities are complex, not only their own, and that these can change over time, they need to understand how our/their identities affect and are affected by social circumstances and historical events and that identities are formed and influenced by many things. This leads to the need to consider not only 'how democracy, justice, diversity, toleration, respect and freedom are valued by people with different beliefs, backgrounds and traditions' (QCA 2007, p. 28), but also how these social processes and institutions are experienced differently by disparate individuals and groups. The quotation neatly brings the three themes together but we need to go much further than that.

While there can be no doubt that identity and diversity are inextricably connected – if we do not all share one common identity then there must inevitably be diversity – it serves neither concept for them to be forever paired. Like rhubarb and custard, or Lennon and McCartney, neither can perhaps exist in our consciousness without the other, but each element has a worth and contribution of its own which we need to examine and understand.

Below we build on and go beyond some of the issues raised by the Ajegbo Report (Ajegbo et al. 2007) to examine the centrality of pupil identities to what they do, how they learn, how they perceive their world and themselves. It is not until schools recognize and allow the development of individual pupil identities that we can expect young people to demonstrate an appreciation of the multiplicity of identities which they will experience in themselves and which they will encounter in others. It is also considering the extent to which the identities of others in the school – teaching and support staff, members of the local community, for example – are supported, explored and celebrated. Kolb (1984) and others have consistently both argued and demonstrated the effectiveness of learning through experience, so that to be exposed to a range of identities can only help young people to understand that there are many more identities out 'there', some elements of which they share and others they do not. One particularly challenging aspect of identity within the Citizenship National Curriculum is the desire to generate an understanding of Britishness; one successful approach to recognizing and addressing the identities which together comprise 'Britishness' is outlined and explained.

Background

Identity is both fragile and complex; everyone with any relationship to a school has an identity made up of multiple roles and elements, not all of which might be recognized or valued by the school. It may be trite and clichéd, but true none the less, to note for example that an adult can be all of teacher, line manager, employee, carer, counsellor, colleague, governor, friend, female, foreign national, heterosexual, faith adherent, political activist, new to the profession, over 40 years of age, sports fixated – and there probably exist other categories not covered by that list. Equally, a young person connected with the same school might be pupil, peer-group leader, volunteer, male, carer, political activist, friend, homosexual, migrant, faith adherent, classical music fixated, and again might relate to other categories not included here. The observation that '[e]ducators need to understand how different identities among youth are being produced in spheres generally ignored by schools' (Giroux 2000, p. 190) applies equally to those adults associated with schools – those with home responsibility for the pupils, support staff, teachers, visitors, governors and a host of others. When teachers are encouraged or expected to relate the content of their lessons to pupils' prior knowledge, this can and should include knowledge gained outside the classroom and away from the school. Otherwise the message is received – whether or not it was intentionally transmitted – that the knowledge and experience of schooling is taken as superior to any other knowledge, any other experience. Any school's first responsibility must be to the pupils in its care, so that to ignore the sources of identities other than 'pupil' is to ignore a part of what makes that person who she/he is.

Pupils have a range of identities, based variously on their own and others' perceptions of them within dimensions such as gender, ethnicity, economic class, self-perception, self-worth, home circumstances, and youth culture(s). Some might be carers for siblings or other family members, others will be cared for by someone of no immediate familial connection. Some will be seen by some teachers to be bright and breezy; the same pupils might be seen by other teachers as lightweight and cheeky. Those seen as gifted by some teachers will be seen as nothing greater than diligent by others, and as 'fooling everyone else but not fooling me' by a few.

Their identities are the outcome of subtle negotiations and liable to even more subtle changes. As teachers we expect (hope?) that our pupils will understand that we are only human, that we also have a home and family relationships to maintain and develop, interests outside work, only 24 hours in the day, a need for a cup of tea/coffee, a need for toilet breaks, a life. Our pupils deserve the same from us. While I would not disagree with Foley (2010) where he writes that '[t]he age of entitlement does not seek character, which demands obligation, but identity, which demands rights' (p. 85), in the context of citizenship education we do not need to be bound by this potential dichotomy but should instead challenge it. A society based wholly upon entitlements is one which will disintegrate through selfishness, while a society based wholly upon obligation will disintegrate through oppression. For teachers and pupils there has to be space both for rights and for obligations, for character as well as for identity.

The previous chapter considered the importance of school ethos and, within that, how the structure and content of lessons and timetables can indicate the citizenship culture of a school. They can equally support the development of positive identities and positive attitudes. Illich (1973) has eloquently shown that, while schools tend to be organized in ways which meet the needs of teachers, this is neither necessary nor desirable. With regard to timetables, for example, we might understand why a teacher prefers a limited number of subject options and a consistent class size, but education has to be about the needs of learners rather than the preferences of teachers.

What constitutes or creates identity?

The 'culturalectomy' identified by Florio-Ruane (2001) and briefly discussed in Chapter 2 is of particular significance to issues of identity. By noting that schools appear to ignore the effects on education of the cultures of the young, she draws our attention to how crucial culture and identity are to learning. In his study of asylums, later extended to other total institutions, Goffman (1961) coined the term 'mortification of the self' for the way in which an individual's identity was systematically dismantled in order for the institution to then make that person present themselves in the way that the institution required. While he was originally discussing total institutions – those which affect their members all day, every day – the principle is applicable to pupils' experience of school, and to other circumstances. Whether we call it culturalectomy or mortification, it is what many schools do and it is not good news for anyone. Halualani discusses at length the limits of 'culture as a knowable entity' (2010, p. 38), certainly in any absolute terms, and the need to recognize that there are tremendous variations in cultural concepts such as 'gender status' and 'social justice', even if we are not able to fully comprehend what these variations or specific interpretations are; at the very least we need to recognize that there are variations, and that individual interpretations are real to those who hold them.

Language can be a powerful identity characteristic, as Labov (1969) and Bernstein (1973) showed in their very different ways, in that it triggers or reinforces certain assumptions in teachers which, in turn, have direct bearing on academic progress and sense of belonging. Labov demonstrated that the complexities of non-standard English, and the multi-linguistic skills of those who use comparable structures in their everyday lives while coping with the standard English of teachers in school and the often impoverished English and another language in the home, are discounted by teachers often significantly less linguistically adept. The social class implications of Bernstein's identification of restricted and elaborate language codes clearly demonstrate that the middle-class values of teachers hold sway in the school. Those teachers who claim to be working class – despite being graduates, with secure white collar jobs, who value educational qualifications, who exercise authority in the workplace – are deluding themselves; there is more to social class than jeans, an open-necked shirt and a few glottal stops. The status and identity conferred by language arises from communal interaction and it is not only the structure of language which matters, the content is vital as well. When Goodman wrote that '[s]peaking is a way of making one's identity, of losing oneself in others in order to grow. It depends not on prior consensus with the others, but on trust of them' (Goodman 1975, p. 70), he was indicating that it is through the interaction of language that we not only learn who we are but also who others think we are. It follows that, if our language or the content of our speech is ignored or ridiculed, so is our identity. That doesn't mean we all have to speak the same way – for to mimic another's accent or speech patterns might easily be interpreted as ridicule – but that we show respect for how others speak, and for what they have to say.

It has been suggested – certainly in staff rooms and governors' meetings I have attended – that a school uniform creates a sense of identity and community, that the wearers can immediately identity with others in the same colour scheme. What a great pity it must be for those young people in France, Palestine, Israel, The Netherlands, The USA, Canada, Germany and so many other countries who have been cast into the wilderness of isolation by not having to wear identical tie, shirt, trousers/skirt, shoes, jacket as others who attend the same school. How terribly lacking in community spirit and a sense of worth they must all be.

The real purpose of any uniform is indicated by the name – to make all wearers of it uniform, to mortify the self rather than to strengthen it. When a student is found to violate uniform regulations they will be punished, the irrelevance of the colour of a pupil's sweater to their ability to solve a quadratic equation or to translate text from one language to another does not matter here; a rule has been broken and so the perpetrator must be seen to be punished.

Pupils quickly learn that it is by being one of the herd – by not expressing identity or individuality – that life is smoothest, safest, easiest in school. Just what the hidden curriculum requires. They also learn, however, that rules exist to be broken, and that it can be fun trying to find increasingly innovative ways to break them.

It is true to say – as many teachers do say – that there are many teachers who have to wear a uniform of sorts to school and that many workplaces impose a dress code on staff. It does not follow, however, that school pupils should wear a uniform. It might be more constructive to question whether teachers should dress as formally as many are required to do, and whether other professions and occupations need necessarily be so determined to remove choice and variety from appearance. There are some types of work where it clearly does matter – those working in sterile, potentially dangerous or in contaminated environments, for example – and it would help pupils to understand why and where it matters if there were discussion rather than a blanket ruling. Another argument in favour of uniform is that so many teen fashions are expensive that it puts pressure on those with low incomes. This might be more persuasive if uniforms were not often so extremely expensive.

There have been many 'debates' – rarely more than editorial diatribe followed by ill-informed reader correspondence – conducted in the UK media regarding whether people should be allowed to wear particular religious symbols at work. Often, these have been part of a not very subtle strategy to create a moral panic (Cohen 1994) over myths that white Christians cannot wear a crucifix while black Muslim women can wear the burkha because Britain is in the throes of some imagined Islamic takeover. The issue of colour is irrelevant here, as Muslims need not be black and Christians need not be white, but it is often a focus in the orchestrated panic none the less.

In relation to schooling, there is no reason why people should not be able to express their faith affiliation. It is unlikely to stimulate argument as pupils will know each others' faith allegiances just as they learn their football team allegiance, their musical genre allegiance, and their fashion preferences. Nor is there any reason why one faith should be given priority over another, or why being a faith adherent is considered better than being agnostic or atheist. Faith adherence or rejection, in themselves, have no effect on learning. There have been Muslim philosophers and mathematicians, for example, whose ideas have shaped much of the modern world, and the case to be made for role models is now well established. Recognition among the non-Muslim population of the positive influences and impact of Islam would also foster understanding of similarities between faiths and differences within them. If we substitute 'Jewish' or 'African' or 'female' or 'homosexual' or 'vegetarian' in place of 'Muslim' and 'Islam' in the previous sentence, we might begin to foster understanding of both similarity and otherness on a significant scale.

(Mis)labelling

Possibly worse than being perceived as part of an amorphous mass – if there is anything worse in the reflections of young people in an affluent society; there are, of course, many things which are far worse in terms of human experiences – is that mass being stereotyped, particularly as anti-social or threatening or unpleasant. Such labels often accrue despite personal experiences to the contrary. When Cohen (1994) describes the process of cognitive dissonance for those who try to balance the conflict between what they see and what they are told thus:

> in a purely statistical sense, the number involved . . . must be a minute proportion of the whole age group, yet so many things that young people get up to today disturb me . . . and who knows what this sort of thing can lead to . . .? So I can't help thinking that this is evidence of a much deeper malaise . . . (Cohen 1994, p. 60),

he is writing about events from the 1960s – the period of adolescence of current senior educators, politicians and grandparents. Either the negative labels were true of most young people but most adults have grown out of such behaviour, or they were untrue of most young people and should therefore be discounted. There is no reason to assume that young people today are significantly socially or developmentally different or will become significantly socially or developmentally different to their grandparents. If the current authority generation held that their identities mattered, it is perfectly reasonable to expect the current youth generation to hold the same belief.

As well as being a matter of principle, of Baldelli's (1971) concept of 'integrity', awareness of the range of identities and their meanings which pupils bring to the classroom and other parts of school has a pragmatic value. When it was reported that 'understanding of multiple identities and allegiances, different and shared histories is important if teachers are to show credibility in their teaching in these areas' (Ofsted 2010, p. 55), a crucial point was being made, one which transfers equally to other parts of the citizenship education curriculum and – in all probability – to all aspects of teaching and learning. If we are to enable and encourage young people to develop awareness of the needs and complex identities of others, it makes no sense to ignore their needs and their identities. If we are going to talk the talk of understanding and recognition of variation and of difference, we need to walk the walk which does the same; there is no place for 'do as I say, not as I do'.

Content matters

It is not enough for schools to provide balance in their assemblies – whether of a broadly Christian nature, whatever that might mean, or not – if they do not consider the content of what they teach and the environment in which teaching and learning takes place. In Chapter 2 we discussed the singular importance of school ethos to the successful development of citizenship education, and it follows from this that subjects must reflect that ethos if we bear in mind the cliché that a chain is only as strong as its weakest link. If it is implied through teaching – either by statement or by omission – that all scientists are men and of European origin, that all artists are men of European origin, that all philosophers are men of European origin, where does that leave Marie Curie, Ben Okri, Confucius, Sappho, Hokusai, Freda Kahlo, and Siddhartha, for example? More importantly, where does it leave those with similar potential and skills who are not being directed to the role models who can give them hope and belief in themselves?

Those politicians and academics who advocate the teaching of a British (in this case, as so often in British life, mistakenly used as a synonym for English) history in England's schools, one which looks only at success and national interest without considering meanings, costs, unequal benefits, power, ethics and repercussions, are trying to instil jingoism and narrow patriotism by depriving young learners of the opportunity to learn about themselves. The intended social engineering is blatant, the principles are questionable, and the intended deceit is disgraceful. Reference to Magna Carta as evidence that Britain was the cradle of democracy ignores that this document predates the existence of Britain as a monarchy by nearly 400 years and as a parliamentary entity by almost 500 years, ignores that it transferred a modicum of power from the monarch to the barons but gave none to the common people, and ignores that there were numerous elected assemblies in other countries long before the Houses of Parliament became in any way either democratic or representative. The histories and roles of the other constituent members of the United Kingdom and of the Commonwealth are thus downplayed or ignored in such an approach to history, as is the radical tradition of Wat Tyler, The Levellers and other opponents of excesses of power, and as is any consideration of the ethics and often destructive effects of imperialism and exploitation. By all means identify and discuss success and development, but we need to present a complete picture to young learners.

It is all very well to praise Wilberforce for involvement in the movement to abolish slavery, but not at the expense of identifying and praising those others who fought longer and harder, and that must not mean Britain's role in the slave trade should be underplayed. By all means discuss and analyse the development of trade and barter with other countries, but the subjugation of people and the exploitation of their resources is part of that process. We should indeed examine developments in science, medicine, the arts and other aspects of human endeavour, but this has to include what women did, what non-Britons and non-Europeans did, what the poorly educated and exploited and impoverished achieved. Everyone deserves to be given the full picture so that they can understand where they are, who they are, and to know something of those around them.

The ill-informed chant of 'one world cup and two world wars' which is dragged out whenever England play Germany at football ignores the latter country's significantly greater success in various international competitions and in head-to-head meetings, as well as glossing over the fact that England has never fought a world war. England has not existed as a sovereign state since 1603 nor as a parliamentary one since 1707. The chant and the xenophobic ranting which has often accompanied it – although thankfully absent during the German dismantling of English football reputations and fantasies in South Africa in 2010 – are a direct outcome of the misrepresentation of history through mass media distortion and school teacher inaccuracy. It is truly the product of ignorance when people do not know or understand their own identities, and it is worth considering why generations have been misled with regard to meanings of English and British.

Case study 3

A major feature of the PGCE 11-18 Citizenship course at Canterbury Christ Church University has been collaboration with school-based subject mentors in developing, planning and delivering collapsed timetable events (focus days) for some partner schools. As well as developing a wide range of student skills and preparing them to be involved in or lead such events once in employment, it also helps to develop other teachers' awareness of a range of strategies and activities which they can usefully deploy with their pupils and therefore strengthen the quality of teaching and learning in those schools.

There is awareness throughout the process of planning, delivery and reflection that collapsed timetable days do not compensate for a lack of adequate curricular provision in school. Breslin (2005) observed that such days can only work when carefully planned by people with appropriate subject specialist expertise and delivered as part of a carefully constructed and sustained programme. In their most recent report on the inspection of Citizenship Education in schools, Ofsted made essentially the same point when recording that 'schools which relied too heavily on suspending the timetable for citizenship were most unlikely to meet National Curriculum requirements' (Ofsted 2010, p. 4). The report goes on to state, however, that 'such days can complement a core curriculum effectively, particularly by providing opportunities for active participation and team projects designed to bring about change' (Ofsted 2010, p. 25). Therefore Ofsted's findings were not that focus days do not work, but that they should be part of systematic curricular development rather than a bolt hole or refuse bin for those things schools might rather not do.

What follows is a summary of the nature of one such focus day which was chock full of active learning and decision-making, and intended to encourage participants and other pupils in the school to reconsider their attitudes towards and perceptions of each other.

The school with which the student teachers worked on this focus day has featured regularly in my published research as 'School A'. It is located in an area of England where the local education authority operates a policy of selection at 11 years of age which directs those identified through tests as in the 'top' 25 per cent of the most academically able to grammar school and the others to high schools. All pupils at the school follow a short-course GCSE in Citizenship Studies and the AS level examination course has been introduced as a popular option. Pupils achieve outstanding academic results e.g. in 2009 almost 75 per cent of A-level grades were A/B and just short of 58 per cent of GCSE grades were A*/A, with Citizenship Studies GCSE grades of A*/A achieved by

75 per cent of pupils in Year 2010. It is therefore not a typical school but, there again, neither is any other school.

Three of the fourteen focus days developed by Canterbury Christ Church University Citizenship PGCE students to date have been at grammar schools, with the others at high schools, an academy and a faith comprehensive. Evaluation of focus days as a strategy (Leighton 2010b) indicates that the type of school is immaterial; what matters is careful and contextual planning. The materials developed – in this case for use with able and motivated year 7 girls, and across the age, phase and ability ranges in other focus days – could be and have been adapted for other circumstances and contexts. Details of the plans and the processes involved in this particular focus day can be found in Knott (2007).

At the time that this particular focus day was planned and presented, School A had discrete timetabled lessons in citizenship as well as cross-curricular provision and a series of focus days. There was a department of two experienced Citizenship specialists as well as many supportive colleagues, a tradition of Citizenship Education which has included giving training places to PGCE Citizenship students since the inception of the course at Canterbury Christ Church University, and a senior management team which was both well informed and fully committed to the development of Citizenship Education.

It was a happy coincidence that the school had chosen 'Britishness' as the theme for a focus day which was delivered in the same week as the Ajegbo Report (Ajegbo et al. 2007) was published. The day was the outcome of a series of meetings between students – face to face and through the university's virtual learning environment – where ideas, strategies and plans were exchanged, discussed, dissected and rebuilt. The process began when the Citizenship subject leader and mentor at School A delivered a session early in the course about the realities of being a student teacher and life in that all-important first post, and to introduce a planning activity. It is that activity which eventually became the 'Britishness' focus day.

The student teachers worked in groups to plan and deliver the sessions, with one student acting as a conduit for ideas and information during planning and as a support and 'gopher' on the day, while another student coordinated activities on the day. The materials which the student teachers developed came from a variety of sources and were particular to that school and those Year 7 pupils. Different schools in different circumstances would be best advised to develop resources appropriate to them. Sessions were presented concurrently so that there are some overlapping details. One way of adapting the plans and principles behind them would be to use them as a unit of work so that all pupils experience all activities.

Case study 3 *Continued*

This would require some pruning as well as a reconsideration of the final session, but should not be beyond the skills of any teacher.

Having been set the task of developing a focus day on the theme of 'Britishness', by the end of a day spent planning the student teachers had decided to divide the Year 7 cohort into seven groups, each of which would work on aspect of the theme in collaboration with 2 or 3 student teachers. Each group would also be supported by a member of the school staff. They decided that each group would be allocated a letter which, when brought together, would form the word 'BRITISH' and illustrate that there are many strands which come together to give a sense of national identity. They decided against making this explicit in the hope that it would become apparent at the final presentation session. There would be a common introduction and discussion, based around a homework task set in advance in preparation for the day, after which the groups were told 'their' theme. They were then introduced to a range of activities which always including forms of research, building towards a presentation to each other at the end of the day.

The letters were taken to represent:

Belonging: simultaneously to the local and the global
Respect: communities that make up Britain
Identity: shared and overlapping identities.
Tradition: traditions from the composite regions of Britain.
Immigration: the origins, diversity and vibrancy of migrant communities and their contribution to Britishness.
Stereotypes: What perceptions do we have of each other, and do others have of the British?
History: what events have shaped our ideas of Britishness and of who we are?

Activities included discussions; identifying origins of clothing; origins of words; music; peer teaching; dressing up; voting; drama; image recognition; advocacy; investigation; fun; acting; online research; artwork; book research; statistical analysis; newspaper research; an adapted television quiz game; writing; radio; and, almost inevitably, powerpoint presentations. Sessions were designed to fit into the school day so that pupils were able to go to break and lunch at their customary times. The biggest difference for pupils was the opportunity to examine an issue in depth and for a sustained period, while both pupils and staff benefited from working with committed subject experts willing and able to innovate.

While such activities can have assessment built into them, and Ofsted (2010) expresses concern that such assessment is not built into focus days often enough, formal written assessment need not and should not be a priority. As focus days should be used to supplement 'a clear core Citizenship programme that addresses the key themes' (Breslin 2005, p. 310), assessment can be more formally identified and recorded in subsequent related lessons. None the less, pupils do have the opportunity for peer and self-assessment when working with others, when making presentation to their group or to the whole year cohort. A focus day makes learning fun, and follow-up activities to this and other focus days clearly indicates that deep learning takes place.

Clearly, not all schools have the benefit of a local university with an available cohort of skilled and committed student teachers of Citizenship Education. Focus days need planning, as do all learning activities. With appropriate forethought and awareness of pupil needs as well as clarity of focus, they can be a highly effective innovation for discrete subjects and for cross-curricular collaborative activities. Although this focus day was specifically for Citizenship Education, it also included art, design technology, English, geography, history, ICT, media studies, religious studies, sociology and theatre studies. Fun, integrated cross-curricular connections, deep learning, opening minds, peer assessment opportunities, collaboration, creativity, a greater understanding and celebration of the multiplicity of factors which influence identity – what more could anyone reasonably ask of one day in school?

Summary

Whoever they are and wherever they are, if pupils bring nothing else to school, they bring themselves. What a wonderful resource for their own and their peers' learning. By building on who our pupils and colleagues are we can ensure that they learn more about themselves and about each other.

4

Diversity

Chapter Outline

Preamble

One of the areas of concern or perceived poor professional preparation identified consistently by those who complete the annual
Newly Qualified Teacher Survey in England – a small, self-selecting
sample which is none the less taken very seriously by the Training
and Development Agency for Schools (TDA) – is that of teaching
in a diverse society. This does not have to be interpreted as a lack of
adequate input and attention by universities or other initial teacher
education (ITE) providers, but could equally represent an awareness on the part of new teachers that there are particularly powerful and complex challenges in responding to the diversity of the
classroom and the diversity of local and national society – and that
there is not always a great deal of similarity between these. The discussion presented here follows directly from the previous chapter
to recognize the complexity and richness of diversity. While attention is given to diversity of ethnicity and some of the ways in which
pupils who find themselves placed outside the dominant culture are

institutionally disadvantaged, other socially constructed categories by which pupils can be identified as different or diverse will be identified, e.g. issues of gender, social class, sexuality, pupils as carers.

Background

One way in which the approach to citizenship education contrasts between that taken in England and, for example, those of France and the USA, is in the attitude to difference. In France and the United States of America considerable emphasis is placed on similarities, on what makes pupils French or 'American' – although, in the case of the latter, there would appear to be no discussion on what binds them to other 'Americans' such as Peruvians, Canadians, Venezuelans, Hondurans, Brazilians, Mexicans etc.. While terms such as African-American and Asian-American have entered into common use in the USA, they are constitutionally considered only to be Citizens of The United States of America. In England there is a conscious focus on difference, effectively an entitlement to being different, at the same time as pursuing that ephemeral and probably non-existent condition known as 'Britishness'. While it has been frequently proposed that this celebration of diversity and difference does little to foster social cohesion, it cannot be persuasively argued that the enforced uniformity model of France or the USA is any more successful in that regard. Indeed, Halualani's (2010) work in the USA identifies an underlying uncertainty among undergraduates regarding their own as well as others' cultures and cultural identities which it is not unreasonable to extend to the rest of that society.

This concept – 'Britishness' – is relatively new and remains largely unformed. When the Conservative politician Norman Tebbitt spoke in the late twentieth century of a cricket team test to determine national loyalties, asserting that immigrants who supported the team from their country of origin rather than their country of adoption were not really British at all, he was really considering English rather than British – a common confusion in the south of Britain, and one which simultaneously does little to help clarify issues and serves to illustrate one of the difficulties in determining 'Britishness', that regional and (sub)national identities are very strong. Former Conservative Prime Minister John Major's eulogy on warm beer and cricket again had an English rather than British focus. In both cases, the notion that cricket is character or identity defining is highly revealing with regard to a particular subnational, and to some extent social class, perception of being British. The complexity of Britishness as an identity is discussed in Chapter 3, and one approach to dismantling and reconstructing it is offered in Case Study 3.

In their discussion of issues of culture and of cultural difference Peters and Bulut (2010) remind us of Willis' work in relation to subcultures, that subcultures are not just systemic but also that it is the exercise of choice by young people to ally with their parental cultures. Before we resort to unsubstantiated generalizations, it is also worth remembering that Preston and Chakrabarty (2010) helpfully show that the choice is not always thus, e.g. despite stereotypes, it is not always the case that young British Asians adopt the values and practices of their parents. Some aim to assimilate while others become more 'traditional', although such traditions vary between faith and region/country of family origin as well as between such regions. As a middle-aged, Scottish-born, secular Jew of multiple national origin, I can confirm that the phenomenon of being pulled in two or more directions is not restricted to young British Asians in present-day England, while Jackson and Marsden (1970) have described and analysed in great detail a similar pressure on academically successful working-class undergraduates.

As discussed in the previous chapter, Britain is a country of multiple identities – as are many other countries to varying degrees – so that recognition of difference cannot sit comfortably with a desire for a single identity. If we consider the informal but widely recognized regional categories in England such as Cockney

(East London), Scouser (Liverpool), Geordie (Newcastle), Brummy (Birmingham), and then add to these the often derogatory images from other parts of Britain such as Jocks (Scotland), Micks (Ireland) and Taffies (Wales), we might conclude that one characteristic of Britishness is diversity, and another is, paradoxically, suspicion and derision of difference. Throughout Britain there are also Jews and Muslim, Sikhs and Hindus, Christians and Humanists, Buddhists and Taoists – and within each of those there are subdivisions and categories of 'other'. There are also people of other European origin as well as Asian, African, North and South American, Pacific, and other ancestries, again with many subdivisions and categories of 'other', and people whose heritage is a hybrid of two or more of these. If we add other variables to this already complex and multidimensional matrix – such as sexuality, age, preference for music, eating habits, computer literacy, social class, social attitudes, gender, employment prospects, attitude to law, attachment (or lack of) to a particular football club – then we could argue that we are all simultaneously very similar and thoroughly unique. However, as Manzoor observed at the conclusion of his account of being a Muslim journalist who had spent a week as a Jew, there is a 'banal but powerful truth, that underneath the skull caps and the headscarves, whether we eat chicken soup or chicken jalfrezi, we really are more similar than we are different' (Manzoor 2010, p. 7). It is significant to remember that so many Britons are the product of variety, and that the specific composition of that variety is permanently in flux.

However, it may be that the overlapping varieties drive us to seek and emphasize difference, not as diversity but as exclusivity. It is over a generation ago that Illich warned us that 'society can be destroyed when further growth of mass production renders the milieu hostile . . . when it isolates people from each other . . . when it undermines the texture of community by promoting extreme polarization' (Illich 1973, p. 11). The increasing uniformity, predictability, homogeneity and standardization of everyday life – the mcdonaldization of existence – is creating false differences to fill the vacuum left by lack of real choice. The differences exist, but the emphasis on them rather than on shared values and potential comes not from within the matrix but from those whose interests are served by a divided society – not only the bourgeoisie and their acolytes, but often also those who wield some level of power within social divisions and who wish to maintain some notional control and status at the expense of the common good. The Marxist concept of divide and rule, where divisions within the proletariat are either manufactured or over-emphasized so that the exploited oppose and compete with each other instead of uniting against a common foe, is clearly applicable here beyond the construct that is social class.

Schools can address this by creating space for recognition of and open discussion about difference, ensuring that citizenship education is about everyone and for everyone. Park (1950) identified ignorance as the greatest contributor to animosity between host and migrant groups; if we change the nomenclature to 'dominant' and 'minority' groups, using access to power and/or numerical presence as our determinants, the same applies. The solution must therefore be to address ignorance; not through some vacuous notion of avoiding offence at all costs but through the informed and reasoned exchange of views which facilitate what has been described as a 'dialogue through disagreement' which leads to people 'finding ways to reasonably disagree' (Smith et al. 2010, pp. 5/6). This means that young people need to be informed – deserve to be informed – and to have the opportunity to develop and express reasoning. Disagreement is healthy and to be encouraged, both for the variety of experience it reflects and for its potential to change minds, and it is best expressed and encountered through dialogue. Discussion around a common theme with common views expressed and disagreement avoided is not a dialogue but a monologue for several voices.

Citizenship education must allow and encourage young people to enter into dialogues, to express and encounter opposing views and learn how to argue their perspective while listening to, understanding, and taking account of others'. Freeman (1995) writes, and Cole (2000) reiterates, that education in Britain allows for very little freedom of expression or right to participation, despite these and other entitlements being laid down in UN charters, conventions and declarations, the European Convention on the Rights of the Child and the 1998 Human Rights Act. A start can be made to rectifying this state of affairs by allowing freedom of expression in the classroom and presenting a forum for participation. For these to be most effective they would have to be replicated throughout the school as part of its ethos (see Chapter 2) as well as responding positively and constructively to ideas and arguments put forward throughout this book. A successful and sustained approach to the development of citizenship education will not be achieved by piecemeal reform and tinkering around the edges; it has to be radical and complete. If we are to teach about diversity and about United Nations charters and Human Rights Acts, it would not go amiss to allow into our classrooms some of the freedoms enshrined in these.

Difference and inequality

It can appear that equality and diversity are mutually exclusive, and that a society which aims to give everyone equal respect and equal opportunity cannot therefore have room for difference and diversity, and this is indeed a challenge. With specific regard to education, Gipps and Murphy (1994) summarize Woods' research in identifying four separate groupings of definitions of 'equal opportunities' which we can scrutinize.

1. *Equal life chances* – which are impossible to achieve unless all life chances are state micro-managed. Such management would have to go far beyond the extremes of soviet interference in schooling, mass media control and the manipulation of political thought, beyond even the worst excesses of fascist states in their extermination of disapproved groups. While many people also experience discrimination in the UK, this does not generally extend to state-authorized

murder. Absolutely equal life chances require a homogenization of social provision, removal of choice, levelling out of income and wealth differences, and a standardization of the gene pool which would be impossible to achieve and, of greater fundamental importance, which is morally abhorrent.

2. *Equal competition for scarce resources* – which might seem appealing but would simply serve to perpetuate inequalities. Those who enjoy advantages by dint of inequalities of wealth or influence already extant would continue to have such advantages and, it can be safely assumed, would continue to make full use of them.

3. *Equal cultivation of different capacities* – this was the claimed objective of the education reforms of the 1940s. For many people the 11+ was or is the ideal but parity of esteem never happened because, while it is possible to regard each human being as of equal worth, some attributes are valued more highly than others. The pressure placed on many primary school pupils in those parts of England where the local education authorities have retained selection, and the amount of money some parents/carers are willing to spend on extra tuition and on launching expensive and emotionally draining appeals, stand as testament to this. While this is not evidence that we cannot celebrate and cultivate different capacities, it does demonstrate the challenge it presents.

4. *Independence of attainment from social origins* – which is unlikely to be achieved in even the most regimented and managed economy. It did not happen in the Soviet Union and it did not happen on Israeli kibbutzim; indeed, Darwinism would suggest it is neither socially desirable nor biologically possible to achieve such independence. We are the sum of our social origins and, while it is possible to challenge or change some of the effects, such challenges and changes are themselves a reaction to – and therefore not independent from – social origins.

Further, we know that reforms in educational provision throughout the twentieth century, whatever else their motives or outcomes, were neither framed nor likely to achieve equality through diversity. Not only in single sex schooling, but even in co-educational establishments, there were different activities for male and female pupils, different play areas and different expectations. Evidence of formal and planned divisions based on ethnicity are less easily identified in the UK, following more a pattern relating to urban migration and zonal location as identified in the USA in the first half of the twentieth century by Burgess and Park, more recently in the UK by Rex and Tomlinson as examples of 'structural breaks.

One exception is the rise of faith schools, lessons about which can be learnt from Northern Ireland, where, it has been argued, there was a consistent and conscious policy of favouritism in provision for the Protestant majority at the expense of the Catholic minority. Those who organized and presided over the educational provision for either side of this divide ensured that children were taught about difference and hatred much more than about similarity and acceptance. Indeed, McGlynn (2004) argued that integrated schooling would stimulate 'natural' acceptance of diversity, while Hayes et al. (2006) found that pupils who had been educated in an integrated system were more likely to lose their traditional and national identities and allegiances than those who had experienced segregated institutions.

Where for most of the last century members of minority ethnic groups who wished their children to learn about their faith were more likely to establish out-of-hours faith schools than to replace or complete with state provision, faith schools now attract state finances. The laissez-faire approach which had contributed to at least tolerance has been replaced, in the face of increasing social division and increasing concerns about ethnic division, to an approach which is based on separation and exclusion. The centuries of evidence from the southern United States, from Northern Ireland and from South Africa tells us that separating people out emphasizes difference and reinforces inequality, which is a far cry from celebrating diversity.

Inclusion

Most schools will claim to be inclusive. While they might mean to imply a largely integrated learning experience for people with recognized and registered disability, inclusion is not the same as integration. Integration is largely about enabling a few pupils to merge with the many. As the Centre for Studies on Inclusion in Education continues to remind us, inclusion centres on increasing the participation of all pupils in all aspects of their local schools. It must be concerned with the full participation of all pupils who might either be considered by others or who perceive themselves to be vulnerable to exclusionary pressures. And 'all pupils' has to really be all pupils.

We know that minority ethnic pupils, and from some minority groups more than others, are more 'vulnerable to exclusionary pressures', as are some economic groups. If 'exclusionary pressures' include bullying – which can result in self-exclusion – then gay pupils, religious pupils, red-headed pupils, Goths and other subculture affiliated pupils, pupils perceived to be overweight, pupils perceived to be underweight, butch, effeminate, sporty, academic, not at all academic pupils are all vulnerable.

> As a teacher you will be expected to provide suitable learning challenges for *all* students, by planning effectively to overcome potential barriers to learning and by responding to diverse learning needs . . . it is about access to the curriculum and to learning for all. (Price 2002, p. 119)

'For all' does not carry any implication of exceptions. In effective, educationally inclusive schools

> the teaching and learning, achievements, attitudes and wellbeing of every young person matter . . . This shows not only in their performance, but also in their ethos and their willingness to offer new opportunities to students who may have experienced previous difficulties. This does not mean treating all students in the same way. Rather it involves taking account of students' varied life experiences and needs. (Clay and George 2002, p. 133)

Considerable media, policy and public attention has been given to the differences in achievement between boys and girls. However, we are reminded that

> Gender is . . . only one factor that affects schooling and achievement. Other factors such as class and ethnicity are strong determinants of educational achievement and thus it is dangerous and inaccurate to imply that all boys underperform and all girls do well. (Clay and George 2002, p. 138)

Research indicates that the gender gap is significantly smaller than the gap associated with class and race:

> of the three best-known dimensions of inequality . . . gender, and in particular boys' underperformance, represents the narrowest disparity. In contrast to the disproportionate media attention, [our] data shows gender to be a less problematic issue than the significant disadvantage of 'race' and the even greater inequality of class. (Gillborn and Mirza 2000, p. 23)

As discussed in Chapter 1, many teachers – and not only teachers of citizenship education – would benefit from appropriate support and development to address areas of concern and self-perceived weakness. Managing diversity is one such area, and Case Study 4 offers one example of some highly effective training. It is the report on a three-year project funded by Oxfam and the Big Lottery Fund between 2007 and 2010 which was conducted under the auspices of the World Education Development Group (WEDG), the Canterbury based Global Education Centre for East Kent, which can be contacted via their website at www.wedg.org.uk. Elsewhere in the UK there is likely to be a similar organization nearby, and there are comparable groups in many other countries; if you have the opportunity you should get in touch and find out what they have to offer, and what you can offer them. Support should be a two-way process, and networking is usually both time and effort well spent.

This case study is included because it gives a realistic picture of what can be achieved and of how much more there is to do. It also stands as evidence that it is possible to address complex issues with very young children, negating the arguments that issues of diversity should be left until pupils are old enough (whenever that might be), and that it is never too early to begin to address such issues. The project serves as a reminder to those of us whose main interests are in secondary education, that there is a great deal of excellent practice taking place in earlier phases and that pupils do not arrive at secondary school experience free. Above all, it draws attention to the need to support and develop staff – in this case, in relation to issues of diversity. The details given below are taken verbatim from the WEDG summary report, and I acknowledge the generosity of WEDG and of Dr Linsey Cameron, of the University of Kent, who conducted the evaluation of the project, for their kind permission to include their findings here.

[The Persona Dolls referred to in the report are widely available and intended to enable trained staff to encourage children to develop empathy with others and to challenge discrimination and unfairness. They are cloth dolls which can be used to help counter the misinformation and prejudice which children might absorb irrespective of the extent (or lack of) their contact with members of a diverse range of social groups. More information, including how to purchase or borrow dolls and how to access training, can be found at http://www.persona-doll-training.org/ukhome.html or from WEDG.]

Case study 4

Attitude is Everything: developing cultural diversity in pre-school education (© World Education Development Group. Reproduced with permission.)

The project

The project took place in three nurseries in Sheerness, Dover and Margate and was based on the idea that building up a positive attitude towards cultural diversity is an essential part of preparing young children for successful lives in the twenty-first century. The project worked with practitioners in building up their knowledge, self-confidence and a positive attitude to cultural diversity which would then be reflected in their daily interactions with young children.

What happened

A major aim of the project was for cultural diversity training to take place in a supportive and enjoyable atmosphere where political correctness would not inhibit questions and discussion. Each setting had a programme that included training,

Case study 4 *Continued*

resources and activities for the practitioners to use with the children. During the training practitioners had the time and opportunity to clarify with colleagues their own thoughts on often difficult and sensitive issues such as terminology and responding to difficult situations.

Cultural ambassadors were recruited, briefed and visited all three settings taking with them food, clothes and other items to show, try on and discuss with both children and adults. This was especially important for practitioners who appreciated having the opportunity to ask questions and clarify their knowledge. By going through these processes practitioners were very definite about their improved self-confidence in how to include cultural diversity in their planning. Many also commented on their increased confidence to address negative comments and actions by children towards others when they arose in everyday situations.

A range of activities and approaches were tested by the practitioners with the children and the best of these can be seen at www.wedg.org.uk.

Objects, photographs of varying scale, games and Persona Dolls were used to introduce aspects of cultural diversity in an engaging and enjoyable way. Each setting used Persona Dolls and adapted the techniques to suit their own situations as circumstances changed. Young children can be harsh judges and with a child-led, freeflow policy in the three settings it soon became clear to practitioners what did and what did not work.

What we achieved

Better Understanding and Awareness of Cultural Diversity Amongst Children and Adults: "You start to be interested in something that really you were never interested in before. Like 'oh that's why they do that' and it breaks down barriers which is the main part of the project isn't it?" (Meadow Nursery Practitioner)

Increased Self Confidence and Skills of Staff: "It came out of nowhere! Suddenly these children were saying things about S's hair and that she looked like a boy. I thought right, time to get out the Persona Doll, before they go home, and it worked! I changed the story a bit of course but they listened and had lots of suggestions." (Shepherdswell Pre-school Practitioner)

Improved Understanding About Racism – What It Is and What It Is not: "You know how to react, more than you did before. You would have been stunned if someone came up with a comment like that before but now, having that input has helped." (Meadow Nursery Practitioner)

Greater Creativity: "Because the children were so interested in the Russian dolls and the way they fitted into one another, we decided to make boxes that fit into one another." (Meadow Nursery Practitioner)

Increased Use of Resources for Cultural Diversity: "Yeah, we've had quite a lot of the photographs and things like that and we've been using those with the children: 'what can you see? What can you see that's the same?' So its making comparisons and chatting. That goes down really well." (Shepherdswell Preschool Practitioner)

Development of Caring Attitude to Others: "Harley is very much a boy's boy. When Lola (Indian Persona Doll) was introduced he really took to her and his usual 'frown' disappeared." (Seashells Sheerness Neighbourhood Nursery Practitioner)

Greater Links with the Wider Community: "An Indian visitor showed the children a toran and explained that in India they are often hung over the doorway as a sign of welcome. The children were proud of their welcome sign they made and parents were interested in the reason for the toran." (Meadow Nursery practitioner)

The wider community

At each setting parents/adults were kept up to date with the project as it evolved through what their children had been doing and the close, frequent contact with staff at the settings via newsletters and notice boards. Although most parental reaction to the project was very positive, at all three settings practitioners reported occasional negative, often off-the-cuff comments about this project or cultural diversity in general. This needs to be taken into consideration in future planning given the close and frequent contact between parents/adults and practitioners.

Spreading best practice

The best learning and everyday practice from the project has been shared with the wider Early Years community. Over 500 Early Years practitioners in East Kent have received training and workshops on successful ways of introducing cultural diversity to young children. This has provided a catalyst for the ongoing development of different approaches, ideas and attitudes within pre-school settings.

The evaluation

The evaluation was carried out by Dr Linsey Cameron, Department of Psychology, University of Kent and aimed to determine

1. Children's attitudes towards diversity and their self-confidence.
2. How frequently and in what way the materials were used by the practitioners.
3. The wider effect on the community, particularly whether it had increased practitioners' knowledge of diversity and confidence in delivering a multicultural education.
4. How WEDG can better support nursery settings in delivering multicultural education.

⇨

Case study 4 *Continued*

Main findings from interviews with children:

- Children made decisions about who they wanted to play with based on the playmate's ethnic background.
- Children were more negative towards some ethnicities than others. Children were particularly negative towards Asian children. Children may have picked this up from social influences, e.g. parents.
- The materials have different effects on boys and girls.

Main findings from interviews with practitioners:

- Practitioners lacked knowledge about diversity issues, e.g. terminology. The project increased their knowledge and confidence in these areas but they still felt they needed ongoing information on different cultures and approaches.
- Practitioners working in pairs when using Persona Dolls were most effective.
- Sharing experiences with staff from other project nurseries boosted self-confidence and generated new ideas

The future

- Must continue to use cultural diversity education resources to develop positive attitudes to avoid playmate preference based on ethnicity.
- Should target interventions at tackling attitudes about groups who are particularly stigmatized in local communities.
- Need to create materials that engage both boys and girls.
- Need for ongoing training in cultural diversity for all settings due to high turnover of staff and low levels of confidence in this area among practitioners.

Summary

The best way to summarize the discussion above is to start with the words of Peter Brett, who observed that

> Celebrating diversity, but ignoring inequality, inevitably leads to the nightmare of entrenched segregation. . . . There can be no true integration without true equality. But the reverse is also true. The equality of the ghetto is no equality at all. Multiculturalism is in danger of

becoming a sleight of hand in which ethnic minorities are distracted by tokens of recognition, while being excluded from the real business.' (Brett 2007, p.3)

We then need to extend this beyond issues of ethnicity to ensure that it encompasses all areas of human diversity, eschewing tokenism and ghettoization so that we can enjoy being safe, being different, and getting on with each other, and perhaps take comfort from the reminder that '[t]here are complex and creative fields of resistance through which class-, race- and gender-mediated practices often refuse, reject, and dismiss the central messages of the schools' (Aronowitz and Giroux 1986, p. 72).

Pupil Voice(s)

Preamble

Pupil voice is commonly trumpeted by many schools as being a well-established component of their citizenship education provision, yet there is rarely compelling evidence that such schools allow pupil voices to be heard in relation to more than the quality of toilet paper, whether uniform should be worn in hot weather, and the colour of the common room. The National Curriculum for Citizenship explicitly states that young people should be encouraged 'to take an interest in topical and controversial issues and to engage in discussion and debate' (QCA 2007, p. 27) and that they should 'learn to argue a case on behalf of others as well as themselves and speak out on issues of concern' (QCA 2007, p. 41). While clothing, common rooms and sanitary arrangements will all rightly be important to young people, we can be confident that there are bigger and more wide-ranging issues of pupils' concern within their schools.

Most teachers' classroom experiences will tell them that pupils can and will ask about any number of issues, often under the guise of academic interest but just as likely to be a ruse to distract the teacher from lesson objectives and learning outcomes. Those same teachers understand that one very effective way to deal with such distractions is to ignore the questions or opinions being put forward, safe in the knowledge that the pupils will eventually tire of asking unanswered questions and so turn their attention to matters which the teacher regards as important, or at least fall into a passivity which allows teaching to take place uninterrupted by pupil involvement or engagement. The same applies to pupil voice. It doesn't take long for pupils to realize that the only opinions and arguments of interest to head teachers and school managers are those which reproduce the opinions and arguments which those same teachers and managers have already aired. Lukes (1974) clearly illustrates how those with authority can manage and manipulate their minions to voice only those statements and opinions which have been approved, while Michels (1949) had previously demonstrated the inevitability of this within his Iron Law of Oligarchy. If we want to facilitate change and enable young people to voice their opinions, concerns, beliefs, prejudices and preferences, we have to enable them to unlearn the hidden processes whereby they express the views expected of them, and to learn to find their own voices. Those voices must be listened to, but it does not follow that everything they express will or should come about. Listening to pupil voices need not always be synonymous with doing what those voices ask.

There are many opportunities for young people to learn how to construct and present arguments, and this chapter examines ways in which pupils can develop their voices and gain opportunities to be heard. It discusses ways in which those in authority in schools can be encouraged to listen, and addresses the thorny yet essential issue of the importance of taking young people and their views seriously while not necessarily always doing what those young people want.

Background

Postman and Weingartner (1976, pp. 131–3) cite a newspaper article from 1967 in which high school dropouts addressing a conference of teachers (an interesting and rarely replicated event) decried the way in which teachers refused to listen to or take account of the attitudes and experiences of the young. No doubt many teachers would say that this situation has been rectified and that we are all alert to the life experiences of the young. Over 40 years later the *Guardian* newspaper carried a report (Williams 2010) from the annual conference of the second biggest trade union for teachers in England regarding a 'debate' which complained that pupils' opinions were being sought with regard to appointments and quality of lessons and that this was 'stripping teachers of their professional dignity'. In 1967 teachers in the USA said they were too busy to listen and that it was their job to teach, in 2010 their English counterparts complained that pupils were distressing teachers and it is those pupils' job to learn – by implication, to learn passively those things which teachers have decided they should learn. It is clear from the second article that, while some of the questions posed by pupils would seem irrelevant or fatuous to some teachers, most of the teacher complaints were about punctured dignity. If pupils think someone with a first-class degree lacks substance or they can render an applicant speechless with a question about behaviour management – two of the examples quoted in the article – perhaps some teachers need to be less inflated with a sense of their own importance. We cannot tell young people to keep quiet until they know better if we don't do all we can to enable them to develop their knowledge – and then we should still not tell them to keep quiet.

Williams's article in the *Guardian* raises another important issue – and not the union general secretary's stated dismay at how unprofessional children can be (what did he expect, adolescent human resource specialists?). Knowing what questions to ask and how to ask them is a challenging skill, and there is no reason to assume that a child's ability to question is the same as her or his ability to ask pertinent questions. As with almost any other aspect of human endeavour, this has to be learnt. Interview panels are one way, practice panels are another. It is clear to anyone who has been involved in interview panels, whether as members or as victims, that young people have not cornered the market in irrelevant, insensitive or nonsensical questions. Developing a range of questioning techniques in classroom interaction and having a range of opportunities to find and develop their voices is the citizenship education route to enabling young people to develop the skill to know what to ask and when to ask it. Any practising or aspiring teacher who finds what children value to be either 'frivolous' or 'demeaning', as the members of that union were said to find those things about which they were asked by children at interview, should question whether teaching is really the career for them.

Democratic schooling

A commitment to pupil voice is a commitment to democratic schooling. This should not be confused with schools run by pupils any more than democratic societies are run by the general population. There is no convincing case to be made for pupils being excluded from all decision-making processes in schools any more than there is a convincing case for pupils to be responsible for making all such decisions. In democratic societies we learn to express our opinions in ways which are governed by laws made by what Mills (1980) described as the power elite. We also learn to participate, to oppose, to conform, to contribute, to work and to make countless daily decisions, again in circumstances dictated by that same elite. To allow pupils to run a school without any authority exercising control over them would not be to prepare them for democracy but to prepare them for a utopian (or perhaps dystopian) world. We can therefore build on Jensen's statement (as Minister for Education in Denmark) '[i]f an education must prepare for democracy it must be democratically organised . . . We don't suggest a connection between democracy and education. We insist upon it' (quoted in Mahony and Hextall 2000, p. 9) to say that such a connection must be realistic and effective.

The future of society depends on generations in development or yet to come, so it is purely a pragmatic decision to ensure that young people are enabled to express themselves coherently and constructively. For them not always to be listened to is to give a taste of reality, for them never to be listened to is to say that they and their opinions don't matter. If they are only listened to when saying what those in authority want them to say, young people will not become acquiescent but they will become disillusioned with authority. The lines between comprehension, concession and condescension must be walked with sensitivity and assurance.

The notion that pupils speak with one voice makes no more sense than television presenters' proclamations that 'the nation has spoken' when some viewers have texted votes for an aspiring music star, and many claims by school managers that they listen to pupil voice – whether school council, pupil surveys, suggestion boxes, pupil focus groups or whatever – are of little more accuracy or value. As Lukes (1974) demonstrates, one of the most effective ways in which debate or dissent can be stifled is to create an illusion of choice, to set and control the agenda. Before considering how to ensure that more pupils are heard, that they are heard more often, and that something comes of them being heard, it is worth considering whether what pupils have to say is worth listening to and acted upon or if it is a) just teenage angst, b) not their role or responsibility to run the school, c) just as well to prepare young people for their adult role of being ignored by those in power by ignoring them from the start.

While enabling pupils to identify and complain about perceived injustices and those things which irritate them are important elements of a radical approach to citizenship education, it is worth remembering and worth reminding our pupils that 'no major thinker has ever recommended or endorsed whingeing. Philosophy from the Stoics to the existentialists rings with denunciations of complaint. Has anyone ever become happier by whingeing' (Foley 2010, p. 90)? Whether or not their dissatisfaction or complaints are justified, the reality is that pupils – just like the rest of us – are more likely to get a response if they phrase things constructively. Much more effective than pupil whinging or strident gainsaying would be to enable them to engage in 'dialogue through disagreement' (Smith et al. 2010, p. 5), recognizing that disagreement is healthy – indeed essential in a democracy – and can be channelled constructively to produce either consensus or, through the process of synthesis, to produce an entirely new idea.

Language

Pupil voices need not only be heard, if they are heard at all, inside the classroom and the school. We do not live in the land of 'Summertime Blues', where elected representatives can get away with being willing to help only those who are old enough to vote – schools can invite local councillors to meet and discuss issues with pupils, as the school of which I am a governor does on a regular basis. Pupils can be encouraged to write to MPs and MEPs, although I recommend that letters should be checked before posting in order to avoid unfortunate consequences.

Few of us respond positively to abuse and being cursed, and it is not middle-class sensibility to expect courtesy and rational argument even in the height of disagreement – it is more likely to get things done, or at least get ideas and disagreements listened to. Pupils will readily accept that they would not like to be disrespected and, through that, recognize that others might feel the same. So we don't – indeed, shouldn't – ask or expect pupils to temper their arguments or change their beliefs, but we must encourage them to understand the benefits of a considered and at least approximately polite approach. If they choose to reject such a strategy that is their choice, but discovering how to get people to listen and take one seriously is part of the process of developing a voice. It is also essential to the continuing place of citizenship education on a school's curriculum that pupils do not commit to paper vituperation and spleen venting directed at the recipient – councillors and Members of Parliament are no happier than anyone else to be on the receiving end of such missives and are liable to make irate and speedy representation to head teachers when they do. That response, and the personal fallout from it, is a part of learning which pupils (and student teachers) might best imagine rather than experience.

Labov (1969) and Bernstein (1973) showed in their different ways that pupil voices are not heard when teachers don't operate on a pupil frequency. Labov's analysis of the language of an African-American teenager, designated at the time as educationally sub-normal, showed him to be eminently capable of abstract thought and rational discussion, while Bernstein demonstrated that working- and middle-class people use different speech codes; the former understood both but the latter only understood their own. As teachers are, by any useful definition and despite any claims to proletarian origins, middle class, this inevitably means that middle-class pupils have an advantage in educational processes – their language as well as their manners constituting parts of what we have since come to know as cultural capital. The pernicious invasion of 'systematic synthetic phonics' into the teaching of reading – as if there is only one way to teach and one way to learn and one time scale for this most essential of skills – is liable to be doing and continue to do extensive damage to generations of readers. I am not an expert in reading or the teaching of it, but it is clear to anyone with the wit to learn from their own and others' experiences that there is more than one way to learn to read, and that many children start school able to read while others do not and might not have opportunities or encouragement at home – their needs are clearly different. However, to control how people learn to read and what they read is also to control how they think, as Dixon (1979) among many others has demonstrated, and to control how they speak and what they speak about is to exercise similar control. It is therefore essential that, while we encourage and enable young people to use the language codes which will get them heard, we do not do so at the expense of their own language and heritage. Work must also be done to enable teachers to better understand those with whom they work and who depend upon them.

Being critical

The ability to make constructive contributions to discussion must be developed as part of radical citizenship education. Rudduck noted in the early days of the National Curriculum that '[t]he critical thinking that fosters scepticism and independence of mind is too much absent from the curriculum' (1991, p. 33) and this seems sadly to be as true over 20 years later. While there is an A level in Critical Thinking, it is not the most commonly offered or taken subject and in any case the experience of critically engaging with ideas needs to begin long before pupils reach the age of 16. There is also an admirable programme called 'Philosophy for Children' – by no means universally present in schools but being increasingly adopted by some, to their credit. Scepticism and independence of mind are crucial aptitudes for constructive and critical citizenship, but they do not sit easily in the teacher psyche; clearly there are teachers who also have some learning to do.

The most recent Ofsted report on the teaching of citizenship education identifies how effective school councils can be in developing learning and understanding when modelled on democratic processes. The report also draws attention to the need to ensure that council members are not passive, but that they are enabled to research into matters of concern to them and that they can campaign for change. Where the report states that such councils 'encapsulated many of the intentions of citizenship education' (Ofsted

2010, p. 11) this should not be read as implying that such councils compensate for inadequate curricular provision; after all, school councils only involve a few pupils for a limited amount of time.

Teachers and pupils can both learn a great deal by pupils having some say in their own learning. Fears that this would result in riotous behaviour and lack of academic rigour are not borne out by evidence – despite allegations, rumours and (other) staffroom myths, learning does take place in Steiner schools and establishments such as Dartington Hall and Summerhill without excessive teacher imposition nor do riots and general mayhem feature in the daily experiences of pupils and teachers. Pupils have a say, teachers have a say, and everyone survives. Indeed, Morgan and Morris write of a need to 'confront [pupils] about their own learning and . . . challenge them to take appropriate actions' (1999, p. 135) in order to enable them to understand the processes as well as the details, and to engage in decision-making which matters to them.

One fascinating outcome of Morgan and Morris' research is in the polarity between pupil and teacher perceptions of the major factors in pupils learning more and learning better. While there are a few reasons about which both groups agree, 62 per cent of teachers think that pupil learning is primarily influenced by the pupil and only 18 per cent that it is an outcome of teaching. The pupils' perspective was that 23 per cent thought it was to do with the pupil but 60 per cent that it was to do with the teacher. Perhaps pupils and teachers should talk to, and listen to, each other more, as they do in those schools where pupils observe and provide feedback on teaching so that teachers can better ensure their lessons are understood by pupils.

We cannot just dismiss young people's opinions say as 'what their parents say' or 'unoriginal' or 'predictable' – there are few people who can claim with any justification to be original in their insights and ways of expressing them. Most of us repeat, adapt or synthesize opinions from those we hear around us, as do young people – it is what socialization is all about, and what maintains the equilibrium of society. It is therefore both harsh and folly to ignore the young for doing what everyone else does simply because they are young.

If citizenship education is to facilitate change and enable the achievement of the aims of the Crick Report (Advisory Group on Citizenship 1998), the development of a generation which possesses and demonstrates social and moral responsibility, community involvement and political literacy, it must not only ensure that young people are informed of their rights and responsibilities but also that their imaginations are stimulated and that they have ownership of their own futures; not a sense of ownership, but real and effective control of their own development. We cannot assume that the young do not already have active imaginations or the skills with which to articulate their views of the present and their desires for the future. Research and observation shows that they have these in abundance.

Case study 5

The young people quoted below might not be a representative cross-sample of their generation, but neither are there grounds to assume that they are exceptional or unique. It is clear that these young people have voices, and there can be no doubt that they have many peers who could be equally vocal; whether or not adults listen to them is another matter. I don't necessarily agree with any of the quotations offered below; that is not the point. Pupil voices represent their views of the world, not something to be edited down to fit an adult perception of what this is or could be. As it says on the homepage of the English Secondary Students' Association,

> [y]oung people are not citizens in waiting. We are here and now. In organising and educati[ng] each other we hold the potential to change a system in which we are not represented. Involving young people is vital to a future that works for everyone. (Rowan Rheingans)

There are very few examples of academic research which has seriously engaged with the views of young people. One study which set out to do just that was White with Brockington (1983), which clearly showed that young people a generation ago were thinking, assessing, criticising and articulating and from which I offer some quotations below.

> 'Freedom is not just within yourself if you're involved with other people. It's something you can only work out as a group, and schools could help you to learn this.' Jo Chadwick (p. 19)

> 'Teachers have to find a way to make it enjoyable for you to want to come to school.' Brian Carr (p. 53)

> 'I'd make teachers pass a second certificate at thirty-five and another at fifty – just to keep them up with the ideas of today. In fifteen years a lot can change.' Leslie Howie (p. 59)

These comments are about school not because that is all young people thought about 30 years ago, but because they are the quotations I selected. They show that some young people have a rather different view of their relationship with schooling than the views which teachers might either hold or expect their pupils to hold. I wonder how many teachers consider how to enable their pupils to engage with ideas and experiences of freedom within a group while making learning a fun experience. For those who don't, perhaps the idea of retraining is particularly appropriate.

Following the 2010 General Election in Britain, some pupils were asked what they would like to see the new government do. Perceptions of political apathy and adolescent inarticulacy would suggest that responses would range from the irrelevant to the incomprehensible. Riley (2010) found the reality rather different.

Libbie Kolokoh (age 6): 'Couldn't we have a web page set up where children can have their say in the country? They need to listen to us.'

Natalie Hughes (age 11): 'We like teaching and teachers to be fun. In our school we are taught how to learn, not what to learn.'

Eduardo Navarro (age 13): 'I want a cleaner city. There is so much rubbish everywhere.'

Ayesha Begum (age 14): 'If schools work collaboratively, rather than in competition with each other, they perform better. It is about the quality of teaching rather than statistics.'

Mohamed Takow (age 15): 'I would like my views to be heard more. I would also like more help for hard-working single mothers.'

Bikesh Rama (age 16): 'If we are to compete, particularly in science and technology, we need to invest in those areas properly.'

⇨

Case study 5 *Continued*

Shareen Khaliq (age 17): 'The idea of letting parents take control of failing schools is an ineffective idea. Many "failing" schools are in deprived areas and parents may lack the cultural capital and expertise to run a school.'

Sarah Sarwar (age 18): 'I want to grow up in a country where the balance of my parents' bank account will not determine my experience at school.'

The Learning for Life Values Poster competition aims to encourage young Scots to reflect upon the human condition and to consider their own core values. In 2006/7 there were over 10,000 pupil submissions from 65 schools. While some adults might scorn or ridicule youthful adoration of celebrity, these young people can justify their admiration of particular people – some of whom are household names while others are family members or friends, fictional characters or ordinary people who have done extraordinary things. Their posters can also include the retelling of stories which, for them, have an important message. More information about the structure of the competition and the nature of the posters can be found at www.learningforlife.org.uk; the quotations are taken from Lorimer (2008), which is largely comprised of extracts from prizewinning entries. Scotland does not operate in years 1–11 but by primary and secondary phases, and the comments are organized here in accordance with that structure.

S1 (12/13 years old)

David McKenzie: 'Learning how to forgive is one thing and that is hard, but learning to be open is another thing that is even harder' (p. 124)

S2 (13/14 years old)

Bhupinder Singh-Sihota: 'To fight for your independence is not a crime.' (p. 63)

S4 (15/16 years old)

Jade Macdonald: 'In a world as messed up as ours, no one can have a hero or inspirational figure . . . because, at some point that 'hero' or 'inspiration' will screw you over to help themselves.' (p. 114)

The quotations identified by the poster makers as worthy of reflection include the following:

Anton Chekhov: 'Any idiot can face a crisis. It is day-to-day living that wears you out.' (p. 26)

Stephen Covey: 'You can't talk yourself out of what you've behaved yourself into' (p. 101)

Albert Einstein: 'Anyone who has never made a mistake has never tried anything new.' (p. 52)

Henry Ford: 'Whether you think you can or you can't, you're usually right' (p. 134)

Mohandas Karamchand Gandhi: 'The future depends on what we do in the present.' (p. 40)

Peter Wentz: 'If you aren't just a little bit depressed, you aren't paying very much attention to what's going on in the world.' (p. 57)

Among the role models and inspirational figures included in posters were the following. If we don't know who they are, perhaps we should, and if we don't know why we certainly should:

Camila Batmanghelidh

Ruby Bridges

Bethany Hamilton

Mary Hartis Jones

Harper Lee

Jason McElwain

Nelson Mandela

Wilfred Owen

Rosa Parks

Jacqueline du Pre

The African Children's Choir

Narayan Toden

Women of the Second World War

Furthermore

If teachers were asked to predict who their pupils would identify as outstanding role models, I do not know who would appear on the list but I am confident it would not be the list above. Similarly, if teachers were asked to identify quotations from the great and the good which their pupils find motivational or inspiring, it is unlikely that many – if any – of those taken here from the Learning for Life Values Poster competition would feature.

Presenting an improving quotation for adult consumption does not mean that a young person has hidden depths or a profound personal philosophy – it could simply mean that they know how to play the assessment game. As teachers we need not only to enable young people to voice their thoughts and to be heard, but also to realize that there are consequence to their voices. If a pupil holds a particular person to be a role model, it is reasonable to expect them to aspire to the same ideals, if they claim to admire a particular phrase there is every reason to look for it reflected in their behaviour. We also need to recognize that there can be other outlets for pupil voices than those offered and managed by the school. An example of this is an article by Sophie O'Connor, written when she was a 16-year-old and about to begin her A-level studies, which appeared in my local free newspaper. It is reproduced here with Sophie's permission and the permission of the Kentish Express Group.

Case study 6

Why am I allowed to work and marry but not vote? (© Sophie O'Connor and © Kentish Express Group. Reproduced with permission.)

At 16 you can start work and leave home – but not vote.

The question of whether or not this is right is aired here by . . . Sophie O'Connor [who] is about to start A levels in history, government and politics, maths and English and wants to go to university and be a writer.

Being only 16-years-old I am unable to vote and, with all of the political mayhem which built up to the election in May, I wish I could be more involved. The shame is that due to my age, the most I could do to have my voice heard is join numerous Facebook groups supporting or scrutinizing policies, parties and leaders. From doing some basic research I have learnt that this is actually quite a predominant political issue. However, each and every article regarding the voting age has been written by a 30-something journalist or political correspondent.

This got me thinking – what do other young people feel about the voting age? After posting a provocative comment on Facebook, I immediately got a response. One 16-year-old commented: "If we are old enough to move out, start a family and begin a career, then surely we are old enough to vote." She was followed by another girl, again aged 16, describing the voting age as similar to "taking candy off a baby". I believe that both these girls raise a good point; if we are supposedly mature enough to form a permanent independent life by getting married, having children and getting a job (which allows us to pay taxes), are we not mature enough to vote?

Many responses suggest that if the voting age were to be lowered to 16, the national curriculum should contain political knowledge. This would install political awareness in us from an early age.

The majority of people who replied to my post were unaware that the national curriculum already contains compulsory units on politics. As the system stands at the moment, only citizenship lessons teach young people about politics, and in many schools these become optional once pupils reach 13.

I was one of the unsuspecting victims to study citizenship at GCSE. I found the curriculum was quite limited. Information on party politics is skimmed across in no detail, thus not satisfying my craving and students' need for a developed understanding of national government.

Political knowledge (or lack of it) aside, why else do people feel that voting at 16 is a bad idea? Many people my age (and often, also older) are incredibly impressionable. One girl who replied to my Facebook post was considerably rude about Gordon Brown with no evidence to explain why she felt that way.

What I feel people must remember is that at all ages there will be a percentage of people who are uninformed and flippant when it come to politics. Similarly, there will also be a percentage of people who are clued up and who genuinely care about politics. Young people are no exception.

Nevertheless, from the numerous responses I received on Facebook, it became quite clear to me that, although there are many mature people of my age who would vote wisely, the majority of adolescents would sooner wipe their rears with their polling cards than vote responsibly.

Summary

There are many voices to be heard in a school, some are rich with insights and advice while others overflow with gripes and grievances; all deserve to be heard but none have the automatic right to be acted upon. Those who are less articulate have to be supported in developing clarity of language and delivery, but we must never confuse eloquence with pertinence or entitlement nor should we forget that, as a proverb puts it, 'Being in the right does not depend on having a loud voice' (quoted in Lorimer 2008, p. 27). In schools we are forever exposed to young voices; we need to ensure that all voices are heard, that all voices are listened to, and that everyone learns how to listen to others, how to express themselves, and how to deal with the consequences.

6

Political Engagement

>

Chapter Outline

Preamble

Citizenship education in the National Curriculum for England came into being because of the enthusiasm of Tony Blair's first Education Secretary, David Blunkett, and the outcome of the report to him by the advisory group he established which was chaired by Bernard Crick. That report tends to be known as the Crick Report, but it was not only an inquiry into a general notion of citizenship education; the full title was 'Education for Citizenship and the teaching of Democracy in Schools: Final Report of the Advisory Group on Citizenship' (Advisory Group on Citizenship 1998), which makes it as clear as anyone might need it to be that the teaching of democracy was and is central to citizenship education. There are, of course, many forms of democracy and many ways in which democracy might be taught. All or any of these models of democracy can be propounded in the classroom and brook no discussion or negotiation – along the lines of 'we are all entitled to our own opinions, don't dare disagree with that sentiment', and 'democracy revolves around freedom of speech – don't interrupt me' – or we can have confidence in democracy, take it seriously and open it to scrutiny.

If pupils are to 'learn about their rights, responsibilities, duties and freedoms, and about laws, justice and democracy' (QCA 2007, p. 41), they will have to engage with the political system, even if only to the extent of trying to gain some understanding of it and even if they ultimately reject it. For pupils to grasp the opportunity, to understand how they can hold to account those in government and others in power, or explore community cohesion, or develop skills of advocacy and representation – above all, how they can take informed and responsible action – requires much more than familiarity with their rights and responsibilities. Once they have developed the knowledge and skills required 'to influence others, bring about change or resist unwanted change' (QCA 2007, p. 45) and put them into practice, pupils will have started to become politically engaged in a formal sense. Many pupils will already be politically active outside of their school lives, through activities such as green and other forms of ethical consumerism.

This chapter builds on ways in which schools can enable pupils to develop political skills and understanding to consider opportunities currently open to pupils to become politically active. This could include party allegiance (but should not be limited to it), considering also pressure and interest groups, starting or supporting local initiatives etc. As a starting point, however, we need to be clear about what constitutes political engagement and to debunk the perception – expressed in the Crick Report (Advisory Group on Citizenship 1998) and by others before and since – of young people as politically apathetic.

Background

To assume that young people are politically disinterested, apathetic, inept or inert depends largely upon one's perception of what constitutes political engagement and what criteria are employed to identify and measure it but, by most rational measures, it is an assumption clearly contradicted by Case Study 6 above, and one which is unsupported by evidence (Kimberlee 2002, Henn et al. 2005). From the USA experience, for example, it is reported that 'it is incorrect to say that young people take no interest in the broader world' (Bernstein 2010, p. 16). On a more global scale, the large sample cross-national study conducted by Ross and Dooly enables them to report that 'children and young people do implicate themselves in political behaviour . . . in contrast to frequent narratives suggesting that indifference to political issues is commonplace among youth' (Ross and Dooly 2010, p. 43).

The commonly held misapprehension that the young are significantly more politically apathetic than preceding generations appears to revolve around the impression of a sudden drop in teenage voting. This is an unreliable indicator in as much as most teenagers do not have the right to vote, and even those aged 18 and over will not always be able to vote as teenagers, given that general elections do not need to occur more than once every five years and that the voter turnout in local and European elections is low for all age groups. Even if we were to accept teenage voting as any more than a snapshot rather than a reliable indicator, it is worth remembering that the fall in turnout is far from sudden as 'voting participation has gradually declined over the past thirty years, and informal political activism has risen sharply' (Ross and Dooly 2010, p. 44). Indeed, their data suggest that, if young people manage to fulfil their own expectations, they will be considerably more active than their parents' generation on all levels.

According to Ross and Dooly (2010), 55.8 per cent of young people expect as adults to vote in elections and another 26.2 per cent consider it a likelihood; 16.9 per cent will discuss politics with friends while 27.5 per cent think they might; 11.5 per cent expect to join campaigns or NGOs with a further 22.7 per cent considering it likely; and 6.5 per cent are certain that they will join a political party and a further 10 per cent recognize this as a possible action as adults. If we combine the 'definites' with the 'possibles', bearing in mind that reality may well lie somewhere between the two, there is a possibility of 82 per cent voting – unprecedented in the UK for almost 100 years. The intention of 17.5 per cent standing for election with only 16.5 per cent joining a political party is an indication of either an as yet naive understanding of how electoral politics work, or of a new politics yet to be established. Even if they do not live up to their own high aspirations, at least these young people have those aspirations and that in itself indicates political engagement. With almost 35 per cent expressing some intention to engage with the political system through campaigning or NGO activity, we are reminded that there is a great deal more to political involvement than the infrequent opportunity to put a mark in a box.

We saw in Chapter 5 that there are many ways in which pupils can become involved in the micro-politics of the school, and that Rudduck (1991) among others has noted the need for schools to do much more to stimulate scepticism and independence of mind through engaging the creative thinking and involvement of pupils. Even in those schools where the teaching and learning of politics is taken seriously, operating wholly on a micro scale does not meet pupils' needs. Indeed, we should be concerned that those schools which enable pupils to develop a good knowledge of citizenship education where 'good knowledge sometimes omitted the central areas of parliamentary government and politics' (Ofsted 2010, p. 9). It does not follow from this that teaching about parliamentary politics necessarily results in a knowledgeable and competent body of pupils, as '[w]here standards were low, students' knowledge was based on completing factual exercises about topics such as parliamentary procedures rather than exploring and discussing current issues' (Ofsted 2010, p. 9). There may be a place for such exercises, although I am at a loss to offer an educationally valid justification for their regular use, but they do nothing to develop understanding or competence, inquiry or independence of thought. There is little purpose and less value to pupils knowing about the colour and categorization of parliamentary papers, the number of readings a specific type of Bill might have to go through, the roles of select and standing committees, simply for the sake of that knowledge; these are things which teachers of citizenship education, particularly the non-specialist teachers, might find out and then present to their pupils as a substitute for teaching and learning about involved citizenship. Of much more use to the pupils, however, would be for them to find out for themselves through inquiry and exploration, and to develop a context for why and how it all works. It is fervently to be hoped that such inquiries will go far beyond naming committees and other easily found, regurgitated and forgotten minutiae.

While it is untrue to allege that all young people are politically disengaged, it would be equally misleading to claim that they are all as astute/cynical as the pseudonymous pupil 'Tory Crimes', who stated that 'A party can say we're going to do this, we're going to do that, and you need to be able to see whether it's possible, or whether they're just talking crap' (White with Brockington 1983, p. 37). There will be young people at either extreme of engagement, with the majority somewhere in between. The extent to which pupils develop politically will be influenced by their domestic circumstances and their peer groups, among a range of agencies, and we should not underplay the significance of their teachers in that development. School ethos will enable either conformity or rebellion – the same ethos can generate either response, as illustrated in the Lindsey Anderson film 'If...' – and pupils deserve a foundation of scepticism and critical analysis from their teachers. After all, '[i]t is unlikely that students will acquire a resistance to propaganda unless their teachers have done the same' (Powell and Solity 1990, p. 6). As Durkheim and other functionalist sociologists have consistently shown, social change is essential for social development, and it comes about through questioning and criticality rather than through meek acceptance; after all '[i]t is through disobedience that progress has been made, disobedience and rebellion' (Wilde 1891, p. 72).

Whose apathy?

One of the three elements of citizenship education proposed by the Crick Report was the development of political literacy, which arose from concern about the 'worrying levels of apathy, ignorance and cynicism about public life' (Advisory Group on Citizenship 1998, p. 8). As noted above, the evidence for the existence of such apathy etc. is sparse to say the least but it would be foolish to completely discount such concerns. Rather than blaming the young for apathy, ignorance and cynicism – a notion which implies that all other age groups are involved, informed and innocently enthusiastic, and that the young are somehow a particularly powerful influence on social mores – it would be more helpful to consider the causes and extent of such attitudes, and to address them. Before doing this it is useful to further clarify what is meant by political engagement and how it can be measured.

The perception that the current young are significantly less engaged than previous generations were, or less than other generations currently are, and that political disillusion is a modern phenomenon, must be examined. Kynaston (2008) cites a great deal of Mass Observation (MO) data which indicate a whole range of attitudes to politics around the time of the 1945 General Election. Bearing in mind that the Mass Observation respondents were disproportionately likely to be middle class, and therefore statistically more likely to be politically aware, two quotations stand out – 'each party running the other down, and when they get in, they'll be bosom pals' (p. 69) and 'Dunno who I'll vote for. I don't like politicians anyway – they're all crooks' (p. 69) – as being echoed in 'Tory Crimes' observation above over 40 years later, and not uncommon another generation further on.

While the theory and some of the proponents of democracy might tell us that everyone is equal in law, in access to power and in social engagement, we know that this is not true in reality. Early in the twentieth century, Weber (2009) explained the need for clear rules and structures, to prevent bureaucrats from assuming the authority of their office and to inhibit their opportunities to manipulate decision-making to their own ends. Michels (1949), a student of Weber, developed his 'Iron Law of Oligarchy' in order to illustrate and demonstrate the inevitability of people becoming more answerable to their hierarchical superiors than to the system which they purport to serve. We know that our political leaders and business directors continue to be more likely to come from a few particular schools, two specific universities, one particular ethnic group, one specific gender, a particular social class – and that they are happy to operate in cahoots with their middle-class, white, independently educated Oxbridge graduate male clones in the mass media and the civil service. When Mills wrote about the power elite, his subject and focus was the formative years of the United States of America but, as with Postman and Weingartner, much of what Mills wrote can be applied to another time and another place – for example, the United Kingdom in the early twenty-first century.

It is not that there are no working class, black or Asian, comprehensive educated, non-graduate women in positions of power – but there are precious few. If we add self-identified as disabled and open about their homosexuality into the mix, as discussed in Chapters 3 and 4, then the numbers will be even smaller. It must either be that all of these socially constructed categories are accurate determinants of political ability – that women are less able than men, that homosexuals are less able than heterosexuals, etc. – or that there is a systemic and institutionalized imbalance in favour of the few and against the majority. This is not what most people would offer as a definition of democracy. To say that young people notice these things is not to offer a startling new insight and can be verified in even the most cursory conversation with school pupils. To deny that they notice imbalances in power is to patronize and to seriously underestimate young people.

The concepts of bureaucratization, of oligarchy and of power elite domination are not simply for sociological consumption. From television's 'Yes, Minister' through 'House of Cards' and onto 'The West Wing' and 'The Thick of It'; the populist and popular work of Michael Moore; news coverage and popular street mythology; we are continually exposed to a perception that the same could be said for capitalist democracy as was often said about state communism – it is fine in theory but unworkable in practice. In its defence we should note that capitalism is generally more colourful, for many it is also more comfortable, and there is a wider choice of television channels.

Politicians

We might ridicule political leaders but they continue to be our political leaders, irrespective of incoherent speech patterns, internecine – and, occasionally, sibling – rivalry, mud-slinging, corruption, double-dealing, deception and dishonesty. We have been told 'there is no alternative' when clearly there are alternatives, that weapons exist when there seems to be no apparent evidence of their existence, that politicians have our interests at heart when many consistently demonstrate the opposite, that they are upright and honest people when evidence is regularly uncovered which indicates that many of them are not. It may be that the perceptions of alternatives, clarity and consistency are not true but, as Thomas' Theorem has it, '[i]f men [*sic*] define situations as real, they are real in their consequences' (Thomas and Thomas 1928, p. 572). In other words, we base our actions on what we perceive to be true, irrespective of the accuracy of those perceptions. It follows from this that, if people believe they are being fed rubbish, they're going to stop swallowing the message;

they may well also bite the hand that tries to feed them unpalatable untruths.

Postman and Weingartner (1976) argued that there is a need for 'a new education that would set out to cultivate . . . experts in crap detecting' (p.16). Teaching is no longer about the dissemination of information, if it ever was. The teaching of citizenship education in particular is about the cultivation of skills of communication and informed participation, the development of both knowledge and understanding of structures and relationships in society, and how such skills and knowledge can be deployed. In order for young people to understand 'what can be' and possibly 'what should be', they need to look at and understand 'what is'. Many of them bring a perception of how life and society operate, rejecting politics in its party sense with its emphasis on economic strategies and the acceptance and admiration of one's alleged betters, while developing interests and opinions on environmentalism, im/emigration, Islam and Islamophobia, concepts of crime and punishment and a range of other political issues. That such opinions might appear partly formed is no bad thing if it means they remain open minded and able to change their opinions in the light of evidence rather than set in their ways and unwilling to consider that which contradicts their long-held but no longer substantiate beliefs. Such young people comfortably fit Postman and Weingarten's (1976, p. 204) criteria for 'crap detectors'.

The perception of politicians that political activity and political literacy are synonymous with voting is one of the areas of crap most frequently detected. Fiona Mctaggart, Home Office Minister at the time, was reported in *The Times* of 20 January 2005 as having declared that society would benefit from a rite of passage for 18-year-olds in which they could assert their commitment to British values and the British way of life, then be given a pocket guide to the constitution and be more likely to vote, showed a marked lack of awareness of many issues – and not only that Britain does not have a constitution to be reduced for bite-sized consumption. It is unlikely that disillusioned or even simply socially self-conscious 18-year-olds would flock to such ceremonies, making it probable that – if anyone does take up the idea – they will be attended by those who already feel committed and attached to society and who are probably therefore likely voters. The notion that there is such a thing as 'Britishness' – for which we might usually be expected to read 'Englishness' – as discussed in Chapter 3, is at best unproven and is clearly at odds with the approach to citizenship education supported by Ms Mctaggart's then colleagues in government. Equally unproven is the notion of any correlation between citizenship ceremonies and increases in voting. If the USA is to be considered an example of oath taking and ceremonial coming of age, their particularly low rate of political participation would indicate that the opposite is true.

The USA has long has ceremonies both of citizenship and to mark the coming of academic, if not majority, age. The consistently low electoral turnout and rarity of underclass involvement in ritualized civic progression in the USA can be taken to indicate that such ceremonies would not be well received; they were not when suggested by Estelle Morris when Education Secretary in 2002, nor when Fiona Mctaggart raised them three years later. There has yet to be legislation introducing them in England and the current likelihood is that, if introduced, they will not succeed. Failure will not be due to the 'unBritishness' of such rituals – after all, many other US-inspired attitudes and forms of behaviour have been successfully transplanted in the UK and elsewhere – but because involvement in them requires and implies some commitment to the values and principles being espoused. For these ceremonies to succeed they would need to have meaning in the lives of the participants; at the moment it would appear that they would have little meaning and no relevance to potential participants.

If politicians are serious about engaging the minds of young citizens, focusing their attention and harnessing their energy, then practical opportunities have to be provided which enable action and engagement rather than passivity and ritual. If school leaders are similarly serious about developing citizens who can play a part in the political life of the country, they must press for and take advantage of those practical opportunities as well as ensuring opportunities exist in and through school for the relevant skills to be practised and developed. In Chapters 2 and 5 above and Chapters 7 and 8 to come, attention is given to a variety of strategies which, as well as involving school ethos, pupil voices, active citizenship and social order, also involve the development of the skills of political engagement. Chapter 9 deals specifically with developing the nuanced skills of identifying what knowledge matters and ways in which young people might apply such skills and knowledge. All of these issues overlap each other, and they coincide with political engagement. The case studies in those chapters relate to provision in the UK; Case Study 7 below outlines two opportunities in Australia which could be replicated in England if the political will exists.

Case study 7

Two Australian programmes which share a focus on sustainability – 'The Australian Sustainable Schools Initiative' (AuSSI) which encourages schools to take systemic, whole-school approaches to sustainability, and 'are you making a difference?' (ruMAD?) – give us some insight into ways in which pupils can consciously influence social order and develop skills which will enable them to continue to do so. It is important to note that these programmes were not established primarily for that purpose in the way that, for example, school councils are expressly to give pupils a voice or that community action projects exist to encourage awareness of and involvement in local communities. The impact on and understanding of political engagement and political change which develops is, in both cases, a by-product of the activity – in Merton's terms, an unintended consequence – which is what makes them so effective and real. Social order and social change do not and cannot exist in a vacuum, but arise from social activity.

Case study 7 *Continued*

Both programmes consciously focus on whole school approaches to sustainability for the simple reason that piecemeal programmes do not work; we can no more be a bit sustainable than we can be a bit pregnant or a bit dead. Participating schools are in a variety of contexts – urban, rural and remote; primary, secondary and straight through; ethnically diverse and mono-cultural.

A common aim for AuSSI schools, like Bradshaw Primary in Alice Springs, is to improve pupil learning and increase pupil engagement in their communities through incorporating sustainability into current school practice. The school has large areas of grass and a number of plants and gardens; it is also in the desert, so water conservation matters to everyone. A school project on water conservation compelled pupils to engage with a current problem likely to become a real threat to them and to their community. In response to this, pupils worked with a production company to make an advertisement about water conservation which was shown on local television, as well as developing three powerpoint presentations subsequently posted on the school website, and reflect real, effective and potentially long-lasting engagement with a locally significant issue. Pupils engaged with a range of people on related trips, they worked in groups to plan and coordinate their activities, they presented their findings at school assemblies. In doing these things they simultaneously developed skills for political engagement and the realization that they could literally make a difference to their community.

Almost 140 miles (220 km) north-west of Bradshaw is Laramba School, with fewer than 100 pupils, all of whom are aged between four and seventeen. Their engagement with AuSSI revolved around horticulture and healthy eating, enabling pupils to make healthy life-style choices and to reconnect with their own culture and traditions. Pupils created and maintain a vegetable garden, have worked with horticulturalists to grow appropriate indigenous trees from seed, and produced a landscape design. All pupils were involved in action planning and decision-making at all times, including what should be planted and where. The benefits of collaboration became clear, and the opportunities to be given and develop personal responsibility readily accepted. Consultation with the community informed decisions about planting to ensure that bushtucker traditions were understood and given an environment in which to return and thrive.

Wondai is a small rural town in an agricultural area of Queensland, dependent on crops and timber industry, so that water is again a very important resource. The school has forests on two sides and a showground on another, caters for 300 pupils from pre-school to year 10, and has a sustainability ethos within which enterprise education is the fulcrum of the school curriculum. The school produces an annual sustainability action plan covering all areas of the curriculum and all year groups, and incorporating a number of local and national initiatives. For example, some pupils were involved in an Earth Dialogues International Forum in Brisbane where, according to one participant, there were debates regarding how economic resources could and should

> be redirected toward the well-needed restoration of the world's forests, oceans and waterways and also to help completely wipe out global poverty. Overall the (Earth Dialogues) weekend was very inspiring to myself and I'm sure to every student that attended, and it made me feel like becoming an environmental/animal/human/ civil rights activist. ('Tully', yr 10)

Tully also wrote an article which was published in a Green and Healthy Schools newsletter, on the basis of which he presented his reflections at the Green and Healthy Schools State Awards teachers' forum. Unlike the Postman and Weingartner (1976) example offered in Chapter 5, here were teachers who would listen to their pupils and who would recognize that education is not all about what 'we' can tell 'them', it is about learning from experiences and from each other. In another activity, year 10 pupils had the opportunity to develop skills for self-sufficiency and collaboration on a large-scale river expedition. One participant commented that

> I've seen things and done things I might not see again. If I could do it again I definitely would and I would recommend it to anybody that gets this opportunity to take it! We learnt how much the pollution changes as you get down the river, how to tell how polluted the water is by the plants and animals living there and how empty the dams are! ('Brielie')

These activities were well publicized by the school, leading to discussions between pupils and community leaders, councillors and the mayor. Pupils shared ideas with others, prepared and delivered speeches, and represented themselves and their community at local, state, national and international levels. They became and continued to be politically engaged; in the words of Sue Gibson, the teacher who coordinated this activity for Wondai School, '"One hand can make a difference, many hands can change the world" and I believe we are in the business of teaching many little hands that they can make a world of difference!'

'are you making a difference?' presents its self as 'a toolkit that enables young people to lead social change and become active citizens. It is focused on values and led by pupils but benefits the whole community' – which is as good definition of political engagement as we might find. As outlined on its home web page, 'At the educational core of this program is a student-centred approach . . . By

Case study 7 *Continued*

being flexible, ruMAD? is also adaptable across varying curriculum and learning environments.' (Lucas Walsh, Director of Research, FYA) and pupils 'learn that they are important today, for what they can do, for the dreams and hopes they hold, and for the changes they can bring about.' (Roger Holdsworth, University of Melbourne AYRC)

At Gagebrook Primary pupils started by improving the local sports ground, then shifted their focus to helping children affected by landmines in Cambodia before deciding to support people less fortunate than themselves and to make a difference to the lives of animals – an eclectic range of activities which reflects young peoples' diverse priorities. Among other activities, pupils conducted interviews, created artworks, wrote letters, circulated a petition, recorded a song, organized activities – including an art auction – attended a conference and spoke in public. As the ruMAD? website states,

> [t]he main focus was on increasing student engagement through positive social action. Students were encouraged to take more responsibility for their learning and thus come to deeper understandings of the community issues they tackled. The process enabled students to develop leadership, life and critical thinking skills. They became active change agents in their own community.

In the state of Victoria, a cluster of six primary schools and one secondary college in Brighton formed a partnership with The Big Issue to raise awareness of homelessness through the lens of sport – in particular, the Homelessness World Cup. Elsewhere in the same state, pupils from Eumemmerring College addressed racism and interethnic tensions by reaching out to local communities to collaborate in building an amphitheatre. They invited local people with appropriate skills to contribute to this whole-community project for which they had to negotiate on construction quotes, plan a conference, deal with local media, and put forward a business plan to the local council. The college's Student Leadership Coordinator, Marina Prassos, summed up the positive impact in that

> [t]heir values (were) reinforced through every activity and I think they'll be better people because of it. After being involved with the Youth Ambassadors Conference, I don't think any of those students are the same . . . they've been affected in a very positive way.

These things to do not happen by accident. There is no possibility of Mickey Rooney turning to Judy Garland, smacking a fist into the palm of his hand, and saying, 'I know! We can change the world, and we'll start *right here*!' Projects and programmes such as those discussed above need funding, they need expertise, they need commitment and time and, more than anything else, belief in the potential of young people. Both of these projects are state funded and supported by expert individuals as well as trained and dedicated teachers. Australia has a land mass almost 60 times that of England, with a population of 30 per cent of England's. If they have been able to overcome the challenges of distance and relative isolation, of rural as well as urban conditions, so can other countries if there is the will.

Summary

Citizenship education will affect pupils for the rest of their lives far beyond the ways in which any other subject will. They will be affected by science but they will not necessarily be scientists; they might speak another language, but only at those times it seems necessary to do so; English and mathematics will exert influences they are not always aware of. Whether they are awake or asleep, at leisure or at work, in the UK or in another country, alone or with family or with friends, they are and will be citizens. All their interactions will be influenced by political considerations, and we disable our pupils if we do not ensure that they understand the possibilities of political engagement and provide opportunities for them to become skilled in influencing their localities and their futures.

7

Active Citizenship

Preamble

Taking informed and responsible action is a significant step towards political engagement as discussed in the previous chapter, and it is at the very heart of a radical approach to citizenship education. As the National Curriculum for Citizenship (QCA 2007, p. 27) reminds us, the Crick Report (Advisory Group on Citizenship 1998) established three principles of effective citizenship education; one of these, community involvement, has to be experienced actively for the simple reason that passivity and involvement must be mutually exclusive concepts. In a properly structured programme of citizenship education there should also, of course, be an abundance of opportunities for young people to become active in relation to the other two principles – social and moral responsibility and political literacy. Active citizenship cannot and must not be exclusively about young people becoming a conscripted army of involved community members – not that there is anything wrong with involvement in the community – as taking social and moral responsibility and developing political literacy both require action on the part of citizens; it is not simply, or even necessarily, about doing things for other people. This chapter is mainly concerned with active citizenship as it relates to community involvement, but the potential for action in other spheres must not be ignored.

Furthermore, the National Curriculum for Citizenship identifies with varying degrees of frequency the following explicitly active approaches to be intrinsic to pupils' experiences and development in learning to become citizens: taking part in decision-making; playing an active part in the life of the school and other communities; questioning values, ideas and viewpoints; communicating with different audiences. As the National Curriculum states, 'active participation provides opportunities to learn about the important role of negotiation and persuasion in a democracy' (QCA 2007, p. 28) and one of the three key processes demanded of the teaching of Citizenship Education by the National Curriculum, along with 'critical thinking and enquiry' and 'advocacy and representation' – both of which offer many opportunities for active learning – is again 'taking informed and responsible action'. This is clearly at the heart of active citizenship.

It should by now be clear that a radical approach to citizenship education, while it might have to take account of the National Curriculum, should be neither limited to that statutory content nor merely a reflection of it. There are many anecdotal cases of pupils being compelled to take part in 'voluntary' activities, or of being directed to participate without the opportunity to discuss, plan or evaluate the activities in which they are participating. The former situation is clearly oxymoronic, while the latter I have described elsewhere (Leighton 2010a, from which the broad thrust of this chapter is developed) as simply reducing active citizenship to a series of worthy acts. Such circumstances arise when teachers have tried to produce evidence that their schemes of work reflect

National Curriculum guidance or to ensure that their pupils meet public examination specification requirements to the letter without taking or being given the time to consider what it is that young people are being required to accomplish, and why.

The importance of active citizenship seems to be agreed upon by teachers, voluntary agencies and politicians. What is less clear is whether those same groups of people agree what the term means either in the abstract or in practice, and it is essential that some common understanding is established. In order to move away from the fixation with worthy acts and the oxymoron of compulsory volunteering, this chapter considers the principle of active citizenship and ways in which schools can facilitate pupils' decisions to become involved. It also draws attention to examples of young people as active citizens outside of their schooling, involved in activities about which their schools know nothing. Active citizenship is not simply about doing good, although it would be unreasonable to oppose good deeds. It is primarily about enabling young people to see that their actions have consequences, that they can make a difference for good if they know how to and choose to do so. The emphasis has to be that we should be most interested in finding ways in which pupils can experience ownership of – and take responsibility for – their actions and the repercussions of those actions.

Background

Opportunities to promote and demonstrate active citizenship in the classroom might not always be easy to identify, but they are there in abundance. We have considered in previous chapters the signal importance of pupils being involved in decision-making at many levels. Case Study 2 illustrates how one primary school has ensured that pupils are consistently aware of their own and others' environmental impact, and how they are enabled to reflect upon and respond to the potential consequences of their actions; that is an example of active citizenship within the school. When pupils work in groups to make decisions, to collaborate on activities, to evaluate their own and others' contributions to an activity, they are involved in active citizenship. Therefore, classroom group work on any topic is an example of active citizenship and both teachers and pupils should be aware of this in developing and celebrating pertinent skills.

Once these and other opportunities are identified, however, it can prove even more of a challenge to engage the support of senior managers and the willing involvement of pupils. In England, participation is not only central to the citizenship education curriculum, it is also an essential component of one of the key aims of the National Curriculum which apply to all subjects – that of making 'a positive contribution to society' (QCA 2007, p. 7) – and making a contribution cannot be a passive process. All teachers, not only those with 'citizenship education' on their timetables, are required to ensure that their pupils are able to take informed and responsible action based on research and investigation, and to analyse the impact of their actions. This is not simply because it is an effective teaching and learning strategy, which it undoubtedly is, but also because it avoids the contradiction inherent in demanding compliance in order to initiate independence – the sort of dichotomy which children of all ages see through and which comfortably fits that category of educational experience described by Postman and Weingartner (1976) as being uncovered by young people's inherent crap detectors.

It is not clear why some educators refer to active participation as this is a tautology. Participation requires some action; to be passive or inactive is not to be involved. Its opposites are either 'active non-participation' or 'passive participation'. The first of these is a clumsy description of the position many people might claim to take, deciding that 'the system' is not for them. This is rarely really the case as such people will generally still be in employment or in receipt of state benefits, pay taxes, interact with their neighbours.

They might have decided not to vote, and their decision is often taken on the basis of partial information or disillusion with the relationship between democratic principle and reality. 'Passive participation' describes the condition in which some people do not openly opt out but equally do not obviously support a given system or aspect of it – perhaps being registered to vote but not voting, or watching a party political broadcast because it takes too much effort to change channels. Rather than become embroiled in a debate which might not yet exist, and which – if it did – would be a distraction from those things which I want to address here, I use the term active citizenship as it represents acceptable custom and some current practice, and bearing in mind Crick's observation that 'it seems elementary – except to some nervous head teachers – that there is a difference between being a good citizen and being an active citizen' (Crick 2004, p. 6). People who are being active are not necessarily performing as citizens – it depends upon the activities in which they are engaged – and those who chose not to become involved can still be good citizens, but they are not active ones.

It should be within our individual and shared competences to find a generally applicable definition of active citizenship, but a significant barrier to this has been identified by Peterson and Knowles (2007) where they found a significant lack of consistency among citizenship education student teachers in England regarding their perceptions of active citizenship as a concept and whether that concept has a shared meaning. In essence, their respondents agreed that active citizenship was highly desirable and that everyone knew what it meant but, on further investigation, the respondents offered a very wide and disparate range of personally held definitions of active citizenship. If this is the case for specialist student teachers of citizenship education, there is a strong likelihood that it could be equally true for those who have already qualified to teach and for those teaching the subject without any specialist background or support. As Peterson and Knowles (2007) state, the National Curriculum guidelines on active participation are clear and they are freely available. They further observe that it does not follow from this that these guidelines are regularly accessed nor that they are either generally discussed or understood.

Purpose

The purpose of active participation must not simply to get pupils to 'do' things, but to enable them to be creative and reflective about the activities in which they become involved – otherwise it is all about 'active' and not at all about 'citizenship'. If such activities are performed only because a teacher says they will be performed, for example because they constitute a public examination requirement or the school authorities see a way of getting something done at little or no expense – or, worst of all, as some sort of punishment – they are unlikely to have any long-standing positive impact. Indeed, the opposite might be more likely. If we want to encourage lifelong participation and involvement, we have to ensure pupils' learning experiences are positive. We must also, therefore, ensure that active citizenship is a learning experience.

To say that the learning experience must be positive should not be misinterpreted to mean that everything should always work out in a pupil's favour, or that all activities are fun and laughter, ending in smiles all round and prizes for all. It may be an unfortunate truth but, as Powell and Solity (1990) remind us, '[r]ecognising you cannot have everything your own way is a painful but essential lesson to learn' (pp. 143/4). Active citizenship, as with all other learning activities, should be geared towards pupils finding things out – about themselves, about their neighbours, about their neighbourhood, their city, their country, their planet. Not everything there is to find out is a good thing, not everything works out to each person's satisfaction. Young people have to learn this as well as those things about themselves, their peers, neighbours and society which might be considered measurable 'facts'. If, for example, they enter a competition in relation to active citizenship, e.g. to run a project which engages with the needs of a particular group in their locality, they might not win; if there is more than one other entrant to the competition, the odds against them winning will increase. An aware teacher of citizenship education will realize, however, that the pupils should have experienced conceiving, planning, delivering and evaluating their contribution – individually as well as collectively – which means that a lot of learning can and should have taken place.

The National Curriculum (QCA 2007) makes it clear that active participation should be both informed and responsible. This cannot and does not mean that the teacher informs the pupils and then either takes responsibility or passes the buck to them if things go awry, but that the pupils ensure that their decisions are informed by research and understanding, and that they are responsible for their actions. Such an approach to learning requires imagination, creativity, research, planning, negotiation, cooperation and, at times, opposition and regrouping. The activity itself should not be mistaken for the purpose of active citizenship, but the means through which pupils learn how they can become involved and the vehicle for assessing the consequences of their actions on themselves and others around them. If pupils are simply forced to do something which people in authority decide upon and monitor closely so that they can all tick a series of boxes and move on, without the opportunity to reflect upon their actions and with no consideration of impact, potential improvements and subsequent developments, they are being put through the motions rather than being given an opportunity to become active citizens. A great opportunity will have been wasted and another group of young people will have been deterred from becoming involved.

Motivation

Motivating pupils to engage in active citizenship can be a challenge, but this can be true of almost any learning experience. Research by Csikszentmihalyi into personal satisfaction indicates that

> teenagers who watched lots of television and hung out in shopping malls, also scored lowest in all satisfaction ratings, whereas those who studied or engaged in sports scored highly on every rating – or on all except one. They believed that the mall rats and couch potatoes were having more fun. (cited in Foley 2010, p. 152)

In other words, some people are achieving high levels of personal satisfaction and others are not, and both groups think the other is having more fun. Leaving aside whether existence can be built exclusively around the expectation of fun, Foley's summary of Csikszentmihalyi's findings indicate that motivated young people will enjoy and they will achieve; the more of them we can motivate, the more achievers there will be and the more they might collectively and individually achieve. If this includes everyone, there will be no 'mall rats and couch potatoes' of whom to be mistakenly envious.

The literature on motivating learners is extensive and not something to be rehearsed or summarized here. However, the immediate function of active citizenship is that it should 'involve, engage and empower pupils' (Davison and Arthur 2003, p. 21), and there is no doubt that people who feel involved, who are engaged in an activity, and who feel positive about themselves and their peers as a result of that activity tend to become highly motivated – it is not the motivation which leads to involvement, but the involvement which leads to motivation. If an activity is decided upon and organized by teachers without involving their pupils at the earliest stages, this activity might somehow still be worthwhile but it is certainly not 'active citizenship'. Such an approach is to be found in teachers' frequent and mistaken belief that active citizenship is just another form of, or term for, work experience or unpaid and unskilled social service provision. This perception serves to deprive young people of their educational entitlement in relation to gaining useful experience of the world of employment and to developing the skills and insights which should arise from active social engagement.

Service learning, participation and worthy acts

Work experience and active citizenship need not be mutually exclusive, however. In considering the British notion of 'work experience' in relation to the concept of 'service learning' prevalent in the United States of America, Lockyer identified an essential difference in that service learning 'involves students engaging in, and reflecting upon, voluntary service in the community . . . the experience must involve reflection and deliberation' (Lockyer 2003, p. 12). Work experience, on the other hand, need involve neither reflection nor deliberation; indeed, insights I have gained both as a teacher and as a GCSE chief examiner would suggest that it need not always involve much work or any useful experience. That service learning is voluntary, engaging and requires reflexivity and deliberation clearly distinguishes it from work experience. Active citizenship requires pupils to take action on problems and issues in order to achieve clearly identified outcomes in relation to them. they cannot do this as part of work experience or work shadowing, where they are expected to find out about the expectations and performance skills associated with a particular occupation or workplace rather than to unionize disadvantaged workers, report breaches of health and safety legislation, or direct a company's profits towards supporting the habitat of indigenous peoples in the Amazonian rain forests. As I have written elsewhere, '[p]upils have to research and plan actions, try to bring about or resist change, offer critical assessments and reflections;

these are skills and processes which rarely if ever feature in work experience diaries' (Leighton 2010a, p. 137). Any event or activity which is planned and developed by teachers or other adults, which does not allow pupils to develop and to learn, is not an example of active citizenship. No matter how worthwhile such events and activities might be perceived to be, and no matter how altruistic the teachers' motives and how enthusiastically their pupils follow instructions, these are – at best – worthy acts, where a short-term good has been met at the expense of long-term engagement.

We also need to question whether such acts are always worthy, just as we should question whether all events planned and run by pupils will necessarily be wholesome examples of active citizenship. To illustrate this with one example of the latter, pupil-run cake stalls which are intended to raise awareness and money for an identified cause can involve a great deal of planning, organization, role allocation, mutual learning, research, informing and motivating peers, costing and various forms of decision-making, and therefore have the potential to be effective examples of active citizenship. They can also create demands for costly ingredients and time-consuming preparation and tidying which falls to those with home-caring responsibilities, who might not have the financial or time resources required. Households with insufficient disposable income, time and skill resources to meet the needs of some grander plans could therefore experience tensions which spill over into the activity and into other school-related relationships, particularly where such activities exist in a 'who can raise the most' environment. These are effectively 'who is the best citizen?' competitions, implying that those who raise the most money are somehow better than those who do not. Pupils selling food will also have an impact on pupil diets and on catering provision. On a large scale such an impact could have a detrimental effect on pupil health and on the employment of catering and meal-time supervising staff. Such activities will have a disproportionately adverse effect on lower income households, and what appears on the surface to be an example of doing good, might well be a case of doing substantial and lasting harm. If the pupils are making and selling cakes simply to raise money for something but not to raise awareness of that something, the citizenship value of the activity is difficult to ascertain.

In order for pupils to understand and reflect upon the activities in which they have been or will be involved, to move these activities from possible worthy acts to clear examples of active citizenship, they need to be aware of the possible consequences of their actions, both intended and unintended. As Merton (1968) identified, unintended consequences can have a greater and more lasting effect that those which we intended or expected. It is not necessary for active citizenship to be world changing – indeed many pupils will be more interested in and aware of their immediate environment – but it is essential that they can identify the possible repercussions of their activities beyond their (or the school's) doorstep. By asking questions and seeking answers, by interrogating their own ideas, pupils will be preparing for active citizenship on a larger and longer lasting scale. Every time a pupil questions the status quo, argues in favour of or against a particular action or event, suggests another way of doing something (which doesn't have to be an inherently better way, if such a thing exists, just a different one), says that they will 'do it differently next time' and can begin to justify any such changes, they are demonstrating active citizenship.

There appears to be an assumption by teachers of citizenship education that active citizenship must mean going out and doing something – fundraising, helping the helpless, tidying the playing fields, bringing about world peace – but this need not be the case. Citizens have their status by being part of society, not by performing good deeds. Active citizenship, therefore, constitutes doing those things expected of members of society – which can include fundraising, etc., but need not be limited to it. Asking question, offering advice, reflecting upon what another pupil says – all of these are examples of active citizenship in the classroom. Some opportunities for participation will arise outside the citizenship classroom but elsewhere in school and provide useful reference points from which to develop pupils' understanding of and engagement with comparable issues. For example, during school council elections issues such as reasons why people decide to stand or not stand; why and how they decide to vote or not vote; how effective the council is or could be or is perceived to be; whether voters are more influenced by the style or the content of election campaigns. These can be related to voting behaviour in local, general and European elections to enable pupils to understand such behaviour and to inform their own future actions; this is one of several cases where we might not see participation until pupils have left school, but we can see citizenship.

Ideal opportunities can arise for active citizenship without planning or teacher forethought, and be particularly useful for their spontaneity. See these rather contrasting examples.

Case study 8

When I returned to school for my final year in 1971, my hair was a lot longer than the head teacher liked boys' hair to be and I had grown what I thought of as a beard. The same was true of several other boys and we were called down to the head's office, expecting to be sent home (if we were lucky) or to the hairdressing department of the nearby technical college.

Instead, we were told that we were each to take responsibility for ourselves and each other. It was explained that the head teacher had no objection to long or facial hair but he had every objection to dirty, untidy or unsafe hair. We were told, therefore, that if any one of us was seen scratching his head, or had a hair-related workshop or laboratory accident, or became slovenly in our appearance, each one of us would have to have our hair cut. I am sure it did not surprise him at all that we became the cleanest, the safest, the tidiest and the most mutually vigilant people in the school.

The head teacher could have given us the usual reprimand followed by the usual temporary exclusion, with the usual lack of sustained impact. Instead, he gave us responsibility for ourselves and each other and a sense that we had been listened to, and we gave a commitment to the school community.

Case study 9

As a teacher I was asked by some Year 11 pupils to intervene on their behalf as they wanted an end-of-year trip but they said their head of year did not think it would be allowed. When I spoke with her it was clear that the head of year had no problem with pupils having such a trip but she did not have the time to organize it. I therefore convened another meeting with the pupils who had approached me and we agreed that they would plan a trip and I would support them approaching the head of year and the head teacher – both of whom I kept informed of developments throughout.

The pupils surveyed their peers regarding possible dates and destinations. They then investigated the costing of the more popular options, taking into account entry fees, coach hire, catering prices – making all contacts with external agencies themselves, using my name solely to lend authority when needed (which it rarely was). The pupils asked school support staff about relevant suppliers, policies, pro-forma and anything else they would have to deal with to satisfy school requirement. Having got all their information together, the pupils again surveyed their peers with potential costs and possible destinations. They also approached staff they thought would be willing and able to accompany them. Armed with their information and planning, they arranged a meeting with the senior management team from which they emerged with permission for the trip to go ahead.

These pupils initiated the idea themselves. They took responsibility. They were doing something for themselves and for others. They had to explain and justify themselves. They had to deal with outside organizations. They had to conduct themselves responsibly. They had to handle money. They had to present a case to people in authority. They gained some understanding of the complexities of others' work. They enjoyed themselves. They had a sense of achievement. They identified, used and developed skills which they could see would be useful to them in life after school. What more could active citizenship, or any learning experience, be expected to offer?

A big society?

There is no reason why schools should limit active citizenship to the classroom or to the school grounds. There are many other social arenas where pupils can be or already are involved. Those schools which require pupils to volunteer to work with or on behalf of others remove the notion of choice implied by the term 'volunteer'. Pupils who decide that volunteering is something they want to do are already involved in active citizenship, whether or not they have actually volunteered. If they can reflect upon why there might be a need for their involvement, the intended and unintended consequences of that involvement, the skills they have developed and the effects of their involvement on themselves and others, then their active participation is particularly secure and impressive. If they just want to do something and have not or do not wish to reflect, it is not active citizenship but it is still to their credit. Many pupils are involved in such a way, and that involvement could become something from which they develop learning about themselves, their skills and the nature of active citizenship.

The UK Government has initiated a pilot of summer schools where young people will come together to work for the benefit of society. These are to be run by charities and will be open to all. As yet, there is no indication whether attendance will be proportionate to the adolescent population by social class, region, ethnicity, gender, physical and mental capacity. I suspect that households which depend upon a school-leaver's income will be less well represented than those which do not, and that those households where a sixteen-year-old is the primary carer will be less well represented than those where this is not the case. It is likely that these Big Society summer schools will break down a few social barriers and enact many worthy deeds, but they do not represent opportunities for social reorganization or active citizenship.

In 2010 senior politicians recommended that pupils who did not get the grades required by their universities of choice should spend some time volunteering instead. How this would help the aspiring student was not made clear, nor was there any apparent discussion about 'volunteering' as a very poor second-choice option. Similarly, unemployed graduates were being encouraged to 'volunteer' for internships with major companies – unpaid work experience which, it was alleged, would prepare them for employment and look good on a curriculum vitae. Unpaid employment is not the same as volunteering. Internships are simply a way in which employers can get work from people in return for nothing at all, and only those with independent financial support could afford such a route to employment. Volunteering is open to all, irrespective of income or academic ability, as it simply requires a desire to get involved and then getting involved. While it is not the same as active citizenship, it can be part of the process.

Schools have a responsibility to develop and enhance community cohesion (as if they do not have enough to do in educating young people). Teachers are required by the National Curriculum for Citizenship (QCA 2007) to take a creative approach to active participation, and to engage their pupils' experiences and imagination. Their pupils are involved in a range of communities, with a greater sense of allegiance to some than to others, and they are much more likely to be willing and able to engage with those communities with which they can identify than with those communities about which they have not heard or which they do not think relate to them. It is by building on their relationships with their own communities that pupils will begin to learn about the communities of their neighbours, then communities possibly further afield. Once they know they have the skills with which to make a difference, it is up to pupils whether they do, how much of a difference they make, and for whom. Six-week long 'doing good' camps might foster some cross-class or cross-cultural bonding or understanding, but they will not and cannot replace the benefits of year-long shared experiences and mutual support.

Summary

There remains a great deal of confusion about what constitutes active citizenship, with the emphasis being placed too often on 'active' rather than 'citizenship'. As with other aspects of citizenship education, attempts have been made to graft an adaption of extant arrangements onto a new policy, amply illustrating the folly of 'innovation without change' (Rudduck 1991, p. 26) which I comment upon in the Introduction. Teachers of citizenship education and school leaders need to recognize that it is the citizenship element which needs to be at the core of such activities, that these should be both about and by the young people involved. People will not know what to do with responsibility if they are never given any, nor be able to apply skills they have not developed. Active citizenship has to be an opportunity – or a series of opportunities – where those skills can be learnt and nurtured.

8

Social Order

Preamble

This chapter reflects upon and develops some of the issues raised in the three previous chapters to assert that social order has to mean progress and development and not social stagnation and repression. Comte's analogy of society as an organism proposes that survival depends upon adaptability; a society which stagnates is one which is dying. We must also recognize that one generation's order and stability is likely to be another generation's moribund strangulation; social order and social control are not synonymous as the former relates to both the nature of society and the relative stability of it, while the latter is concerned with who controls, manages and benefits from the nature and degree of social change.

While there could be a perception that 'social order' and 'radical' are mutually exclusive concepts, this is far from the case. Challenge and change are at the centre of the radical approach to citizenship education, enhanced by an understanding of what is and what might be and, in the wonderful definition attributed to Raymond Williams, the recognition that 'to be truly radical is to make hope possible rather than despair convincing'. This has to include an understanding of the current social order and what maintains social order, how to question these and – if and where they are found wanting – what alternatives might be considered, for social order means both the maintenance of an orderly and regulated society, and an established social hierarchy. If the regulations of society are open to question, development and change, as they must be in a democratic society, so must the social structures upon which they depend.

When the National Curriculum for Citizenship requires that 'pupils learn about their rights, responsibilities, duties and freedoms and about laws, justice and democracy' (QCA 2007, p. 41) it is requiring scrutiny and understanding of social order. When we 'equip pupils to engage critically with and explore diverse ideas, beliefs, cultures and identities and the values we share as citizens in the UK' (QCA 2007, p. 27) they expose the established social order to scrutiny and gain an understanding of social change. To avoid such examination of the nature of society and of social change suggests that we either do not trust young people to understand how things are and how they have come about, or we fear that our society does not bear scrutiny. Neither position is tenable – education cannot be built on distrust and fear, but on honesty, cooperation and confidence.

Background

As an undergraduate I appeared in a play which retold the story of the followers of the ancient god Dionysus, who were sometimes known as the Bacchae, priestesses of ancient Greece who had a penchant for excessive drunken revelry. Playing the part of a senior civil servant, my first lines referred to Thebes' ordered society in which work and recreation each had their time and place, and where citizens had homes and the opportunity to have a say in the running of society. That the play is not more widely known says much more about the limitations of my acting skills than it does about the talent of the playwright, but the message that some things are constant remains true. Ours is still an ordered society, there are times and places for work, as there are for recreation, and many of us have some say in how things are organized and run. That is not to say that society is unchanged and unchanging – after all, the work we do, the pastimes we might enjoy, their times and their places are all very different in twenty-first-century Britain than they were in pre-Common Era Thebes – but that changes do take place in stable and well-managed stages. They have to so that social order changes without becoming long-term social disorder, so that society develops rather than stagnates.

One of the concerns which gave rise to the introduction of citizenship education was a perception that social order was breaking down. There had been demonstrations, sometimes characterized as violent, in relation to industrial disputes, the 'poll tax', road developments, 'New Age travellers' and wars in the preceding decade. A young black man Stephen Lawrence was murdered in South London by white youths who were never brought to justice, and a young white boy James Bulger was murdered in Liverpool by two children not very much older than their victim. Philip Lawrence, a London head teacher, was fatally stabbed when intervening in an argument outside his school. Newspapers were regularly reporting increases in violent crime, possession of knives and firearms. Engagement in traditional political activities such as party membership, trade union membership and voting in elections appeared to be at their lowest point for many years. The political establishment was alarmed at what it perceived to be a rending of the fabric of society, and felt it necessary to address such serious damage before it became irreparable. Whether there really was a breakdown of social order is not something which was then exposed to particular scrutiny, and we must consider whether that interpretation of circumstances is an accurate one.

For events such as those outlined above to truly constitute potential disaster, they would have to be unusual in both nature and frequency in relation to former times; this was not and is not the case. The miners' strikes of the 1980s and 1990s were in response to a clearly stated government policy to take on and destroy the power of trades unions. There is little evidence that this policy was other than successful, with violent clashes between police and striking workers not being a characteristic of industrial unrest in the last decade of the twentieth century. It is far from clear that the violence was the product of strikers' behaviour and aggression, given the well-documented taunting of miners by police, and the stated police strategies of isolating and intimidating strikers. Such conduct by those who were expected to protect ordinary citizens, plus the limitations placed on personal mobility during the strikes – with motorists from active strike areas being prevented by police from travelling to other parts of the country – is, if evidence of anything connected with social order, perhaps indicative of an oppressive and increasingly martial state rather than of a disintegrating society. By the 1990s, there were few industrial disputes and even fewer examples of anything other than placid and highly controlled industrial protests.

Signification spiral

The Crick Report (Advisory Group on Citizenship 1998) offers two of the murders mentioned above as evidence of social disintegration among the young. However, Stephen Lawrence's death, no matter how tragic and distressing for those who knew and loved him, was not a freak event in as much as there was roughly one murder each day in the United Kingdom that year. The mass media, however, raised the profile of this killing above all the others; other killings which resulted in other tragedies and others' distress. The focus on Stephen Lawrence might have been a media reaction to the victim being apparently well-liked, academically able, respectable and responsible – in other words, he did not fit the media stereotype of young black men. The *Daily Mail* placed itself at the forefront of those newspapers which decried this murder and offered it as evidence of social decay – going so far as to run a front page which named as guilty those thought to be suspected of the murder by the police and calling on the men named to sue the newspaper if the statement was untrue – before returning to its more customary vilification of immigrants and non-whites which remains evident today.

James Bulger was a four-year-old boy enticed away from a shopping centre while his mother's back was momentarily turned, then brutally mistreated by his ten-year-old abductors before being murdered in 1993. Again, the mass media raised the profile of this killing above others before and since, as if it were one example of a particularly pernicious social trend, and continues to do so. There was considerable media and public pressure for the murderers to be given exemplary punishments, to never be released from prison, to be made to suffer. There seemed to be scant consideration given to the nature of a society run by adults that can produce children who commit such horrific crimes, and a lot of attention given to how to punish two particular perpetrators. No evidence was offered that 1993 saw an increase in juvenile murder (it didn't) nor that young black men had suddenly become victimized by young white men (such victimization was certainly not sudden). There seems also to have been precious little discussion about young people's much greater likelihood of experiencing violence, including unlawful killing, at the hands of adults. This whole process of media identification of a problem – whether youth apathy or youth crime or youth whatever-an-editor-decides-to-condemn – is sometimes referred to as a moral panic or media amplification but, while both concepts are relevant and possibly applicable, it more closely typifies the 'Signification

Spiral' described by the CCCS Mugging Group (1975, p. 77). An issue is identified and, with it, blame is heaped upon an alleged subversive minority. The initial problem issues are then linked to other problem issues so that further escalation appears inevitable, often in the UK with explanations and prophesies invoking parallels with the perceived decline of social cohesion in the USA. Then there is a call for strong action. A raft of sociologists throughout the 1970s, most prominently Cohen (1971, 1994), Young (1971), and Hall and Jefferson (1975), outlined and critiqued this process to identify the manipulation of public consciousness towards some 'renegade' aspects of social misbehaviour and away from the questionable conduct of those of run and manage society. This is not to say that all such news is necessarily manufactured but that it can be and is frequently distorted, creating a fear of circumstances which far outweighs their extent or probable impact.

Cohesion

Social order, as with most aspects of social existence and all aspects of citizenship education, is an apparently straightforward concept which operates on many levels and in many ways, making it a much more complex and dynamic process than it might first appear. Preston and Chakrabarty (2010) make the point that social order depends upon social cohesion and that there can be conflicting systems of integration which can simultaneously enable cohesion within a group and threaten order in wider society. Therefore a group of people, simply by dint of being a group, can simultaneously be integrated within and by themselves – be orderly – and yet present a real or perceived danger to the social fabric. The virulent Islamaphobia of much of the popular media is predicated upon this being true for some if not all Muslims. Previously, and with at least a little more accuracy, the same process of simultaneous internal cohesion and outsider threat could have been identified in relation to the Red Army Fraction in Germany, Brigado Rosso in Italy, and The Angry Brigade in the UK, for example, groups whose threat to society and whose internal cohesion was considerably less than the media portrayal.

Significantly less violent but none the less equally accurate examples of this phenomenon are the political developments of Scotland and Wales within the UK – not, perhaps, a physical threat to the UK, but certainly a threat to the Union. A radical approach to citizenship education does not require that all pupils are encouraged to take an oath of allegiance to the state and report to the thought police all those whose loyalty is questionable, even though such oaths have been suggested by a series of Education Secretaries and other politicians (see Chapter 6).

When Preston and Chakrabarty (2010) observe that there can be conflicting loyalties, they do not suggest such conflict to be inevitable. There are many groups to which members feel loyalty while also being law abiding, accepting of society at large, and generally little threat to anyone. Indeed there are some organizations, such as the Scout movement and Neighbourhood Watch groups, where group identity can help to foster wider social cohesion. There are, of course, also examples of group cohesion reinforcing social cohesion to such an extent that there is a real or perceived threat to social order – the more extreme club and subnational football fans being just one example. It is therefore essential that we strive to facilitate a social order which is not nationalistic, exclusive, chauvinistic or narrowly focused but one which celebrates and values difference while sharing what is common to all.

Such a shift, from the familiar to the unknown, is much more likely to appeal to the young than to the old. In part this is because the old tend to become more conservative, wanting to protect what they have and fearing the unknown. The young, on the other hand, see the mess they are likely to inherit from the old and recognize that anything would be an improvement. This is not new; it was thus when my generation was young, when my great-grandparents were young – which is why they migrated to the UK, to get away from situations and circumstances they wanted to change but could not. When Oakeshott, doyen of the oxymoronic 'radical right' in the UK, proclaims the superiority of 'the tried to the untried . . . the convenient to the perfect, present laughter to utopian bliss' (Oakeshott 1962, p. 162), he does not appear to consider whose convenience is best served, whose laugher rings out, when processes and objectives remain the tried and established. It is unquestionably in the interests of the older, the white and the more powerful that things do not change, while it is in the interests of now and the future that they do. Foley (2010, p. 5) offers an account of the deliberations of the Gross National Happiness Commission of Bhutan, describing as 'lamentable' the perception that young Bhutanese 50 years ago would have chosen the king as their hero whereas now it is the rapper 50 Cent. It is an odd state of affairs when someone expresses concern that the young prefer their heroes to have achieved status through talent and to speak to them in ways and about things which connect to them rather than idolizing a hereditary monarch whose only achievement is an accident of conception. The preference might be viewed as either one of the negatives of globalization or evidence of incipient republicanism but, whichever interpretation one prefers, it is clear that the social order in Bhutan is shifting, even if both more slowly and more suddenly than in some other societies.

We currently live in a society where young people, predominantly black young people, are being shot at in chip shops, on the street, at family celebrations, in their homes. It is little wonder therefore that they have limited faith in the current social order. That those who carry out the shooting might also predominantly be young and predominantly from minority ethnic groups serve only to emphasize the extent to which those members of society feel suspicious and alienated. The media amplification of these and similar events distorts their frequency and increases people's perceptions of their likelihood, and it is this fear of becoming the victim of violence which motivates and informs our social attitudes and social behaviour, and which the British Crime Survey reveals is most apparent among minority ethnic groups in the UK who accurately perceive themselves to be the most likely victims of violence.

Fear of violence and victimhood of other crimes, limited educational opportunities, restricted employment opportunities in terms both of the number and the nature of job available all militate against young people feeling positive about themselves and about the current social order. For many of those who might have a less fearful outlook, a reluctance to both incur a huge debt and face higher rates of taxation deters some from becoming undergraduates, thereby limiting both their opportunities and the benefits which would accrue to society from the maximum development of socially desired skills and attributes. If the traditional choices look bleak, it can be little surprise when young people opt for alternatives which place them in a vicious cycle not of their making. Some politicians might claim that we are all in this together, but it is clear that 'our society as presently structured will continue to generate problems for some of its members – like working-class adolescents – and then condemn whatever solution these groups find' (Cohen 1994, p. 1 and p. 204).

Although a fictional character developed by a writer who is also a teacher in Morrall's 'The Man Who Disappeared', 12-year-old Millie reflects a truth for adults as well as making a telling observation about school life when she says that 'unwritten rules are much more important than written ones' (Morrall 2010, p. 35). Much later and with equal prescience, Millie also notes '[t]hat's how you get new ideas, people thinking different things, not agreeing' (Morrall 2010, p. 375) and surely most of us would recognize that the alternative to new ideas and change is dependence on old ideas and stagnation. We need new ideas and members of my generation need to reflect upon our discomfort with these – whether we fear the idea itself or simply its newness.

To suspect or fear the new simply because it is new or because we do not understand has no more merit than a pupil refusing to learn something because they have not already been taught it. As adults, whether teachers, parents or other carers, we know that young people will have to encounter things for the first time. We expect them to deal with it and we offer guidance and support to help them to do so. The same has to apply in reverse – if we as adults encounter a new idea we should have to deal with it, and might have to seek the guidance and advice of the young to manage. If the idea is to be rejected because we have considered it, dismantled it, have evidence which undermines or contradicts it, then we are engaging with the idea in the way that we would expect our pupils to engage. If we fear the idea because we don't like the change it might bring about, such fears should be aired but they are not in themselves a reason to expect others to reject the idea.

Those who want to bring about change are always a nuisance – just consider the irritation which Jesus and Mohandas Gandhi caused to the authorities of their times – but they are essential.

> Agitators are a set of interfering, meddling people, who come down to some perfectly contented class in the community, and sow seeds of discontent amongst them. That is the reason why agitators are so abundantly necessary. Without them, in our incomplete state, there would be no advance towards civilization. (Wilde 1891, p. 73)

If we want to ensure that such an advance is ordered and effective we must not attempt to silence our pupils and stifle discussion. Much more effective will be to enable young people to practise the skills they need to identify those things they wish to change and then to effect those change they desire. This can be done in a number of ways as discussed above and as shown in Case Study 10, which outlines the approach to social order and ordered social change established at Denbigh School in Milton Keynes.

Case study 10

Denbigh School has some 1400 pupils and has been described by Ofsted as having outstanding effectiveness, with the rationale of 'doing what is best for each student' (Ofsted 2009). Of particular relevance to us here is the observation that pupils 'have a vested interest in its success, respect each other and are proud of their school. Their voice is heard extensively in all manner of developments, including helping in the drive to improve teaching and learning' (Ofsted 2009). As has already been shown (see Chapter 5) opportunities for the expression of pupil voices are essential to equipping young people to bring about orderly social change. At Denbigh, the opportunities are more extensive and more varied.

Pupils volunteer for training to provide peer mentoring, which serves three purposes: it creates a sense of security and well-being for mentees, a sense of purpose and achievement for mentors, and a school community which is comfortable with itself – and which is an example of active citizenship. There is also a learning partner programme through which pupils observe lessons and feed back to teachers their thoughts on what seems to work and what does not, and why. Pupils and staff are trained in this relationship so that all parties benefit; it is not a case of pupils managing the teachers or teachers designing lessons to court popularity, but a programme intended to ensure that everyone gives of their best and maximizes the benefits available to them. There is no doubt about who is in charge, but this is not based on a fixed or zero-sum theory of power. Teachers and the school management team are confident enough in themselves and in their pupils to be willing to engage in discussion and be open to suggestions for change. This openness and confidence not only provides pupils with an opportunity to contribute ideas and observations – it challenges them to do so. Pupils have long complained about this teacher and that strategy, those text books and one approach or another. Instead of exchanging complaints and endless whinges, secure in the knowledge that nobody is listening to them so they can be as irresponsible and negative as their imaginations allow, the pupils at Denbigh have to face up to the realities of the classroom and to what can be achieved. The right to become engaged in managing their learning carries with it the obligation to be effectively engaged.

There is a school council which is elected via nominations, manifestos and a school-funded election day. It meets weekly to manage its budget and to monitor the progress of its projects and priorities. There is a house system in the school, and each house has a similarly elected council which works closely with the school council. This avoids one of the major problems of school councils, of a relative concentration of influence and experience in the hands of a few – usually older – pupils. Councillors serve for two years, ensuring continuity while allowing

Case study 10 *Continued*

change. There is also a series of 12 satellite groups evolved from and reporting to the school council, concerned with the school governing body, behaviour, citizenship, uniform, recruitment, teaching and learning and a range of other activities covering all aspects of the school. In this way pupils can come to understand the complex community of which they are members, and constructively contribute to its development. Ofsted (2009) described the school council as 'a key force . . . through which the school seeks students' views and actively responds to their concerns . . . (giving pupils) a clear message that the school wants to treat them respectfully and listen to their views'. All pupils in Milton Keynes benefit from a website run by school pupils on behalf of the City Council, ensuring that it is informed and that young people express their views and concerns. This clearly includes Denbeigh pupils, whose links with the local business community are extensive and have been recognized by local and national awards.

Pupil opportunities to engage in orderly change go beyond school council, house councils, satellite groups, mentoring, learning support, charity activities and representation of the governing body. After all, not everyone can be elected or selected, not everyone has the time or the desire to become involved in such activities. The school website draws pupils' and other browsers' attention to individual and group achievements by pupils – in sports and performance, as well as community and academic activities – as well as being a source of information about numerous activities which offer a window on the wider world.

An insight into the school's weltanshauung can be found by examining its website from 27 September 2010. That day was identified as National European Languages Day on which Denbigh adopted Turkish, with facts and phrases links available online. Also listed for September were World Reflexology Week and the Jewish festival of Sukkot. Indicated as on their way for October were Black History Month, Breast Cancer Awareness Month, International Walk to School Month, International School Libraries Month and World Blind Awareness Month. A wide range of active or commemorative events offered without judgement or detail, serving purely to remind everyone that there are lots of different people and interests beyond the confines of the school, lots of opportunities for involvement and many ways in which to try to make a difference.

The philosophy which underwrites the broad and detailed approach taken by Denbigh is summed up in the head teacher's welcome '[t]he school fosters personal development that helps students to find meaning in their lives and respond with creativity and determination to the challenges that arise through the rapid pace of social change'. The social order is changing, and here we have an example of one school's approach to ensuring that such change is managed in an orderly fashion and that its pupils are equipped to manage it effectively.

Summary

We know from experience and from current circumstances that social order is in a permanent flux. To pretend otherwise is to delude ourselves and to deceive our pupils. We therefore have a responsibility to them to enable those pupils to understand the nature, rate and processes of change in the social order, and to equip them to play the part they wish to play in shaping that change.

Some school leaders might fear – or at least argue – that this can only happen at the cost of schools' primary responsibility, that of maximizing examination performance. Denbigh School clearly illustrates that pupils can develop the skills and awareness demanded to be able to shape social order and social change without jeopardizing examination results. There is even a powerful case to be made that the approach at Denbigh reinforces pupils' academic work and strengthens their achievements. The point must also be made that schools' main responsibility is not to maximize examination performance but to educate pupils so that they fulfil their potential and, with a bit of luck, for the good of society.

Political Knowledge

Preamble

Political knowledge is not synonymous with knowledge of politics. A truism has it that 'knowledge is power' and, as politics is the organization and exercise of power – and, if we're lucky, of responsible authority – political knowledge is knowing what knowledge matters, when it matters, how to find it and how to use it. Gobbets of information such as why seats in the House of Commons are green and those in the House of Lords are red, or why the Speaker's Chair used to be a commode, might win points in pub quizzes, prizes on television game shows or marks in classroom tests and public examinations, but they don't really matter.

Citizenship education can and should provide access to what Apple (1990) refers to as powerful knowledge, rather than simply being the transfer of facts about civics from the forefront of one person's brain or lesson plan into the recesses of another's brain or rarely read notepad. This chapter brings together some of the knowledge implied or explicitly raised in previous chapters. The relative places and merits of 'content' and 'skills', much discussed in teacher education, are scrutinized as we bear in mind that it is impossible to generate worthwhile discussions among and between pupils unless those discussions are properly informed and about something, that '[g]ood discussion cannot take place in a vacuum' (Ofsted 2010, p. 14).

While often well meant, the outcome as much of misplaced good intentions as a lack of wit or imagination, there are many teachers who seek to provide 'the truth' to pupils – and pupils often seek such truth, even (or particularly) where it does not exist. Rudduck identifies crucial and complex issues regarding political knowledge when she writes that

> teachers and pupils often conspire in perpetuating a false security that manifests itself in a reliance on right answers and on a view of the expert as one who knows rather than one who uses knowledge to refocus doubt. Teachers, prompted by a kindly concern for those they teach, often over-simplify the complexities of living and learning; they seek to protect their pupils from uncertainty. (Rudduck 1991, p. 33)

Such protection is short term and exceedingly harmful as it inhibits intellectual curiosity, subscribes to the myth of omnipotent expertise, and deceives pupils into believing that there exist right answers to all things. Blake et al. (2000) have explained that learning must develop the potential for emotional engagement while, for Geelan (2010), an awareness of ambiguity and the ability to face up to and deal with it is crucial. Such engagement and awareness can combine to equip pupils with the tools necessary for the acquisition of political knowledge.

Background

The content of the National Curriculum for Citizenship, as with all other National Curriculum subjects, was decided initially by civil servants and ultimately by Parliament, following a consultation process with teachers and their subject organizations. A significant difference in the case of Citizenship Education is that there was also an advisory group appointed by the Secretary of State for Education to identify appropriate knowledge and skills to meet the aim of extending and encouraging democratic and responsible involvement. As with Hargreaves' (2004) otherwise very encouraging and often perceptive discussion on the need to consider the aspirations and expectations young people hold regarding their education, and despite the insights offered and the example set by White with Brockington (1983) and Morgan and Morris (1999), one important group not included in the discussions about what young people think and believe, what they know, do not know and possibly ought to know, was the young themselves.

One of the main concerns of the Ofsted (Bell 2005a, 2005b; Ofsted 2006, 2010) has been the way in which citizenship education is delivered in schools with what often appears to be only a cursory relationship with National Curriculum requirements. Structures of delivery have been addressed elsewhere (Leighton 2002, 2004c), but a common approach is to see the subject combined with Personal Social and Health Education (PSHE), or with Careers Education, perhaps once a fortnight. It therefore becomes a subject perceived as of little academic value and little valued by the school, taught largely by non-specialists, and considered at best an irrelevance and often a distraction from the 'proper' business of schooling. At least one school has moved from 'Citizenship' to 'Life Skills' in response to pupils previously changing the final letter to a 't', others offer PACE (Personal and Citizenship Education) or some other locally created but not necessarily even locally understood name.

There are many ways in which pupils can and do develop their political knowledge. Following on from Case Study 3, one such way is briefly outlined and evaluated below.

Case study 11 (© Philip Tutin. Reproduced with permission.)

We constructed a carousel of five different workshop activities on a range of issues related to sustainability and global environmental responsibility. Pupils had advance notice of the activities and were asked to sign up to a first and second choice. The workshops ranged from 'Bin Bag Fashion' (a creative activity relating to sustainable clothing) to 'Fossil Fuels Forever?' – a discussion and planning session about consequences and alternatives in the energy industry.

Focus days were a major part of curriculum at the school and also a very valuable one. Teaching staff were assigned every second Friday to a year group and focus event; they were not a flagship event that necessarily guided the building of the school calendar but an integral part of the curriculum. It could be argued that their effectiveness might therefore be reduced, as students succumb to routine and boredom; however this was not the case. Students find such days interesting and a welcome break from the routine of their own timetable. With specific reference to citizenship education, such days give the pupils chances to explore the subject in ways they might not have conceived as relevant or possible in their classroom lessons. The cross-curricular links with the work we did with them on that day were self-evident, but pupils often struggle to see the relevance of the subject within the confines of their regular citizenship education classes.

The themes of Science, Art, Design and Conflict Resolution were central to the pupils' experiences on our focus day, more than just vehicles for us to address the citizenship education aspect of the topic. Some people regard the best citizenship education as that which cannot be identified, traced or marked out, like an implicit theory of learning you might say . . . and what better way for students to develop into rounded, knowledgeable and informed adults who are able to make links with thoughts, actions and consequences across myriad issues and dilemmas, privately and publically, as well as locally and globally, than to have them regularly engaging in focus-day type exercises?

In my experience, the more you expose students to learning scenarios outside the classroom, the better they are able to contribute to, understand and take advantage of the learning opportunities being cooked up by teachers in them.

For the sake of government statistics on the number of children getting A*–C in some token of formalized qualification in citizenship education, we shouldn't be reducing it to a discrete subject that happens only in the citizenship education classroom. You can hear kids around school refer to that room as the 'CE classroom' and even that teacher as the 'CE teacher'. . . . soon followed by the question, 'CE? What the f**k is that?' Sadly, followed by the same old answer . . . 'dunno exactly'. Citizenship education teachers should all want to change the world. . . . and I think the boundaries of that world should extend to the whole school. Philip Tutin, teacher of Psychology and Social Studies at John Port School, Derbyshire

Developing political knowledge

We have already identified that many schools advocate school councils and community action projects; there are others which promote general studies and general lectures on aspects of current affairs. Schools also provide career guidance and information regarding sexual health, substance abuse and legal responsibilities. These activities tend to be controlled by teachers who either set their own restrictions or follow guidelines laid down by school managers or school governors; as Illich (1973) argued, they are organized to meet the priorities and needs of teachers rather than those of pupils.

Despite the example set by Denbigh School outlined in Case Study 10, it is exceptional for a school to devolve any budget to a school council, although a few do; it is rare for schools to have pupil representation on governing bodies, although there is legislated provision for such representation. It is almost unheard of, in the state sector, for pupils to have any formal say in the structure of their day, their lessons or their curriculum. What is worth knowing, therefore, in preparation for adulthood and participation in the rights and responsibilities which constitute being a citizen, is almost always dictated according to Bowles and Gintis' (1976) 'Jug and mug' principle – that those in authority believe they know best and they pass on whatever knowledge they deem suitable in whatever format meets their preferences. This hidden curricular message, self-evidently not a universal truth to anyone with any sympathy for a radical approach to any aspect of education, produces a widespread attitude of opposition to citizenship education because of the inherent hypocrisy of an approach which says 'we will tell you what is important to you, how to form opinions and what opinions to form'.

Lawton (1975) makes clear that 'different disciplines ask different questions' (p. 74) and that 'schools have often only succeeded in differentiating between disciplines at the cost of ignoring the relationships between them.' (p. 74) Over 30 years later, the

National Curriculum for England (QCA 2007) finally made it an explicit requirement that the relationship between subjects must be identified and developed in teaching and learning – which surely must include more than just where they consider different aspects of the same thing, e.g. when physics and geography both consider volcanoes, or physical education and biology look at health. Understanding how subjects interrelate, and how other aspects of pupils' knowledge matters, must be an objective of citizenship education and one route to the development of political knowledge in order to establish and nurture the abilities to sift and to synthesize.

The underpinning values of citizenship education include that it enables the development of skills of enquiry, the ability to form and articulate personal opinions, to understand the views of others, and to prepare young people to play an active and effective part in shaping the type of society in which they wish to live. Foisting a passive acceptance of the status quo is an improbable route to achieving these objectives. Rather than placing an emphasis on a body of 'facts', a more appropriate approach is to enable young people to understand society and how to read society. In the words of Postman and Weingartner, 'in order to survive in a world of rapid change there is nothing more worth knowing . . . than the continual process of how to make viable meanings.' (1976, p. 85)

Guesswork

This brings our attention to whose meanings are considered to be viable or worthwhile. Postman and Weingartner clearly had their own agenda for viable, appropriate and worthwhile, but it cannot be claimed that there is a universal purpose to teaching nor a uniform perception of meaning. They propose a range of different teacher 'types', each of which I can people from my experiences as a pupil, as a teacher and as a teacher educator. There are those who want to illuminate, or want to cultivate; those who want to keep minds busy, or strengthen them, or fill them up; those who want to mould, or to feed, or to provide a firm foundation. While this variety may well be preferable to a 'one-type-fits-all' approach to teaching, it is not without its drawbacks.

For pupils, part of the reality of the process of schooling will be to be able to identify which 'type' best describes a particular teacher then to work out and apply whatever strategies will bring most success in appearing to meet that teacher's criteria. This perception follows on from the findings of Hargreaves (1967), Willis (1977) and Corrigan (1979) among many others. 'Successful' pupils, therefore, could be those who can most effectively judge and meet the expectations of a teacher type. Those who are equally successful at judging but either do not have the strategies of apparent or real compliance, or prefer not to employ them, are unlikely to be successful. Those not equipped or unwilling to make effective judgements might find that they hit upon a coping strategy which sees them through the system, or they fail to do so and therefore struggle through the system. If this is what is happening in citizenship education lessons, where they exist, then those lessons become simply another part of the process of negotiating survival rather than part of the process of skills and knowledge development.

If this is the case then, inadvertently, pupils have learnt to make viable meanings and act according to them – a valuable citizenship skill. However, they will have learnt how to be manipulated and acquiescent rather than how to be discerning and assertive. A systematic and coherent approach to developing similar skills and discernment, but without creating a long-lasting antipathy to education and to authority, would be a more productive and socially effective strategy in the long run.

Postman and Weingartner (1976) argue that much of pupils' involvement in the processes of education has been based on guesswork – they are expected to guess how apparently disparate strands are interconnected, and guess what answer the teacher wants, as well as guessing what is might constitute truth, which varies between teachers – but with the valued questions, the values behind the questions, and arbitration on the validity of the invited guesses, being in the sole remit of teachers.

At their time of writing, and still the case today in some highly influential quarters, questioning this dependence on guesswork has been rejected as 'trendy' or 'progressive' as 'most educators . . . are largely interested to know whether it will accomplish the goals that older learning media have tried to achieve' (Postman and Weingartner 1976, p. 37). The point that they were making was that this is the wrong test; as the truism has it, 'if you do what you have always done you will get what you have always got'. While this approach would fit the philosophy of conservative writers such as Oakeshott (1962), it is far from one which will encourage, enable and facilitate progress towards developing the skills required for survival by individuals and societies in the twenty-first century. New methods of learning and development are necessary for new skills and a change in the nature of society. It is through questioning not acceptance, working things out instead of learning by rote, cooperating rather than competing, that new attitudes will be forged and the needs of a more rewarding society will be met. It is surely healthy that consistent exposure to questioning has developed a desire to question.

It is telling that 'trendy' and 'progressive' are pejorative terms in education. In other environments it would be considered helpful to be up to date with current trends and developments and to be forward looking and forward thinking but not, apparently, when considering the development of young people and the future of society. This might reflect a fear of inquiry or a fear of uncovering inadequacy among decision makers and commentators, a preference for their own feelings of security and superiority rather than looking to develop and enhance the prospects of future generations. Bowles's and Gintis's (1976) Correspondence Theory might lead us to conclude that such decision makers and commentators are determined that young people are not encouraged to have questioning, enquiring and critical approaches but, instead, should be acquiescent and accommodating.

Citizenship education must be about being questioning. It has to aim for pupils to being informed enough to know which questions to ask and of whom they should be asked, and being alert to the consequences as well as the content of any answers. Asking directed and informed questions is one of the 'utilitarian skills' derided by highly tradition-bound educators such as Chris Woodhead, a former Chief Inspector of Schools and the first head of Ofsted, whose emphasis on knowledge as a collection of irrefutable facts assumed either that teachers can give pupils all the answers or that teachers and the National Curriculum must have absolute control over what constitutes appropriate knowledge. This approach ignores that teachers do not universally applaud all that is in the National Curriculum, that the National Curriculum in many subjects has emphasized skills as well as knowledge in order to give a context to what might be known, and – perhaps most crucially – young people are asking questions and probably always have done.

Case study 12

It has been noted that 'Clear ideas are the surest bastion against fraudulence and malicious nonsense' (Baldelli 1971, p. 25). Enabling young people to develop clarity of thought, and articulation of such clarity, must therefore be a key objective of citizenship education. One way to achieve this is to encourage and enable pupils' involvement in debates in the classroom and beyond, to support them in the development of skills of research and analysis, of organizing ideas and evaluating them, of considering data and selecting from them. There is a wealth of debating clubs and competitions which might appear to develop such skills, but we need to be wary of those which are more concerned with style than substance and to concentrate our attention on those which emphasize clarity of thought and the

Case study 12 *Continued*

marshalling of evidence-based argument. One particularly constructive approach is illustrated by Debating Matters.

Many classroom debates are little more than ill-prepared and poorly presented arguments based on opinion, a quick web search and a few points gleaned from the mass media, with perhaps a few questions from equally poorly informed friends. Some schools try to compensate for these sorry episodes by establishing highly formulaic and procedural debating clubs in which pupils learn how to try to be polite to each other while offering slightly better prepared and presented arguments – again based on opinion, a quick web search and a few points gleaned from the mass media – with questions both planted and predictable. Both approaches miss an opportunity for young people to learn how to find information, how to assess what is useful to an argument and what is superfluous, how to organize their data, how to predict and contest opposing positions, how to ask and respond to searching questions, and how to improve on all these skills. In other words, they fail to equip pupils with the skills required for what I have called 'political knowledge'. It is not always straightforward to identify what knowledge will be useful in our lives or how it will be useful, but we can at least learn how to marshal our knowledge and decide what is relevant and when. One way to do this can be found at http://www.debatingmatters.com/.

Debating Matters began in 2002 when David Perks, Head of Physics and convenor of the debate society at Graveney School in South London, suggested a competition to focus pupils' attention on the intellectual content of current debates rather than on rhetoric and sophistry. The key aspects of the format he proposed which can contribute to the development of political knowledge are: the early provision of debate motions and allocation of positions for or against, which encourages thorough preparation; the central role of a panel of diverse judges in cross-examining the speakers about their opening statements, and providing critical feedback; the opportunity for speakers to engage with each others' arguments; and the importance attached to audience contributions, so that everyone is involved. Central to the success of the debates has been the topic guides, freely available on the Debating Matters website, which offer reliable data and summaries of key arguments and therefore demonstrate the value of in-depth research.

It might be tempting to dismiss Debating Matters as simply another public-speaking competition for highly academic sixth formers, but this would be a mistake on several levels.

1. There is little simple about it;
2. There is a world of a difference between public speaking and debating; the former emphasizes oratory and rhetoric, the second is much more concerned with the ability to argue a point of view;

3. There is also a difference between Debating Matters' format and those of other competitions. Debating Matters places the emphasis on content over procedure, and on substance over style; it encourages young people to engage in the exchange of ideas and exposes their arguments to scrutiny. The stated premise is that debating matters because ideas matter;

4. Why dismiss competition? If we are preparing our pupils to play a part as citizens, we do them no favours by pretending that everyone is a winner in all things, nor need it mean that those who do not win should have a big L branded onto their foreheads;

5. The format can be adapted to develop the skills and meet the needs of virtually any group of pupils, not only the academic and certainly not only older ones.

6. It is a format which takes ideas, argument and young people seriously.

The competition currently involves almost 200 schools throughout the UK, and has twice been awarded an Engaging Science Society Award by the Wellcome Trust. Previous participants have taken up internships, chaired debates, prepared topic guides, briefed judges, and generally demonstrated how much participation in the debates has meant to them and helped them to develop.

The structure is clear and rigorous, but it is neither rigid nor context bound. Debating Matters runs a similar competition in India and has developed regional variations in Northern Ireland and, in conjunction with Peninsula AimHigher, for younger pupils in south-west England. Further developments have included working in partnership with the Research Councils UK (RCUK) as part of their 'Global Uncertainties: Security for all in a Changing World' programme, and with Newcastle University's year-long Changing Age programme, looking at the medical, moral and social issues society needs to consider with an aging population. My own involvement began when I ran a three-week residential citizenship course for 13- to 16-year-olds on behalf of the National Academy for Gifted and Talented Youth (NAGTY) in the summer of 2003. Some schools – not only those who participate in the competition – have adopted the format for their own debating societies.

The heats, regional finals and national final of the competition are the best illustrations of the benefits to young people of the structure and processes involved in debating in this way, and I recommend teachers and pupils to attend these if possible or, failing that, to watch the video clips or DVD available online. Speakers know well in advance what their topic is and where to find information on it – and where those speaking for the other side of the motion can find their information. As well as speaking, questioning and responding to audience questions, participants have to deal with questions from an 'expert' panel. The

Case study 12 *Continued*

panel's questions are unpredictable, which necessitates speakers understanding their arguments and the bigger picture surrounding the topic, and it is the panel which decides who has won – thereby avoiding victory going to the team with the most friends in the audience. Judges are also required to explain their decision, which results in praise, criticism and advice.

Debating Matters includes in its short-term aims, to provide training opportunities and educational support that leads to continuous improvement in the quality of the debates that pupils engage in and assists schools and pupils new to debate to try Debating Matters out, and to encourage greater debate activity within schools and greater interaction between schools outside of the formal framework of the Debating Matters competition. In the longer term it aspires to foster intellectual curiosity and rigour and to create an environment which encourages deeper levels of knowledge and understanding about political, social and cultural issues as a precursor to generating new thinking and ideas about solving problems in new ways. In other words, it is about enhancing the quality of political knowledge and citizenship skills.

There are topic guides on a number of pertinent debates, many of which some teachers – and some pupils – might initially regard as too complex or too demanding. It has been my experience, and the experience of the Debating Matters team, that young people rise to the challenge. Topic guides are available online and are under the following headings:

- Arts and culture
- Health and medicine
- Environment
- International relations
- Liberty and law
- Media
- Politics
- Science and experimentation
- Sport and leisure

There is no reason why this approach cannot be put into action in schools, as at least one of my former students has done and other teachers are doing. Tom Finn-Kelsey at Queen Elizabeth Grammar School, Faversham, has adapted the Debating Matters structure effectively enough for his school to come second in the national competition in 2009/10, for a considerable number of pupils to have become involved in regular school debates, and for pupils to organize and run those debates without Tom's close involvement – serving both to allow the pupils autonomy and avoiding adding to Tom's workload. The number and success of pupils studying politics at A level also reflects the benefits of Tom's approach and his pupils' enthusiasm, commitment and development.

While challenging to achieve this without the involvement of dedicated debate organizers, it is not beyond the skills of most teachers. Judging panels could comprise teachers with areas of interest which relate to the topic, e.g. 'In sport, winning is everything' could involve PE staff, 'Clinical trials in developing countries are exploitative' could involve science, geography and RE teachers, but pupils will learn most about the whole process if they also feature on these panels. By involving teachers from departments other than Citizenship or English (wherein debating commonly resides), pupils will learn how everything they do in school is interconnected and staff will learn that they are involved in citizenship education. Having been involved in many such panels, I have found them to be stimulating, hard work and lots of fun. Once they are shown what is involved in planning and understand that they really do have the skills and authority to take on the responsibility of planning and running such debates, pupils leap at the opportunity.

Pupils can be paired across year groups, friendship groups or however seems appropriate. As the debates and their distinctive format become familiar, new pupils will learn from the more experienced – and the more experienced will learn from their new colleagues as it is a format which gives everyone a voice. Topic guides will continue to be available, which means that the hardest part for a teacher – enabling pupils to get useful information together in the first place – has already been taken care of, although there is no reason why teachers, and pupils, cannot conduct further research. If a local significant topic is not covered by the guides, the experience and expertise developed from extensive use of those which do exist will make developing new ones so much easier.

By collaborating over research, speeches and questions, pupils develop social awareness and the ability to work with others. The topics themselves demand that pupils learn about a range of matters, and that they understand what they learn. Panel questions show that they are taken seriously and put them under pressure, while panel advice helps them to develop. The debate topics help them to place their everyday learning in practical and applied contexts, demonstrate the value of research and preparation, and enable them to develop a wider understanding of views which they not only might not hold but of which they might not even be aware. My experience has been that young people respond positively to the demands of the Debating Matters structure. Try it and see.

Summary

Bits of information which can be easily looked up in a reference book or online wiki site do not constitute powerful knowledge, and the teacher who simply passes on such information is not being much help to anyone and certainly not teaching anyone or anything. Enabling pupils to find and understand such information is much more useful to them as well as much more interesting for the teacher. Most important of all, however, is the development in pupils of discernment and judgement, of articulation and insight, of argument and objective. Knowledge is only power when it includes how and when to use it, and an understanding of what it means.

What Next?

Preamble

Either side of briefly recapping the central arguments of Chapters 1 to 9, this final chapter considers how a radical approach to the teaching of Citizenship Education might shape the subject. The question in this chapter title must lead us to further areas for discussion and development within citizenship education. We need to continue to ask questions of ourselves, of the subject, and of each other; questions about radical approaches to assessment which will meet pupil, social, teacher, school and policy needs and aspirations; questions regarding the development of a forum to share ideas and strategies, nationally and internationally, and to remind radical citizenship education teachers that they are not alone; questions about how we can work with like-minded colleagues in other disciplines, and how we can reach and work with colleagues who feel too nervous, uninformed, ill-informed, ill-equipped or ill-advised to understand and make full use of the opportunities provided by citizenship education to enhance the skills and life chances of all our pupils.

Discussion

It would be foolish to pretend that we know what the future holds. Nostradamus had the wit (or perhaps I underestimate his talent and it was foresight) to make his predictions both so vague and so numerous that he could be held equally to have foretold so much or nothing at all that has come to pass. Less obfuscating forecasters have not necessarily been any more successful, finding that predicting the future is a fraught and thankless business. People invent things, or discover things, or develop easier (sometimes more difficult but seemingly easier) ways of doing things. Expected pleasure turns out to be unmitigated disaster, impending doom transpires to be less disastrous than expected. One party in government lays down what it perceives as the framework for communal bliss, only to be replaced by another with a different view, a different blueprint, perhaps even a different perception of bliss. If, however, we do not think about future possibilities and probable developments, we are likely to make a complete mess of things – the evidence of that is all around us. Therefore, we need to hazard a guess at what the future holds, and to suggest ways to make it work.

Kynaston (2008) captures the almost tangible excitement and positive outlook prevalent in post-war Britain; the Welfare State was imminent, urban renewal was underway, there was a sense of social opportunity and social equality in the air. He also observes that such euphoria was extremely short lived. A generation later, social commentators such as Rattray Taylor (1977) were predicting the collapse of telephone services worldwide, gridlocked traffic the length of the country, and acts of international terrorism as a daily occurrence. He ridiculed any possibility that the UK would have had a female prime minister by 2000, and concluded that, basically, the world was going to hell in a handcart. Writing from a politically different standpoint in the USA, Toffler (1973) was more hopeful but still concerned for his equally inaccurate image of what the future held, yet the pictures they drew a generation ago of the dystopian world which would greet the twenty-first century are not so very different to predictions being made now for the near future. They got some things right but, as with Postman and Weingartner's (1976) list of problems discussed in Chapter 1, things might be bad but they haven't become as bad as predicted. There is no reason, therefore, to think that current doomsayers are any more to be trusted or any more likely to be accurate in their forecasts.

Schumacher (1974) held out much greater hope than many of his contemporaries and, I do not believe it to be co-incidental, considered the importance of education in much greater depth than either Toffler or Rattray Taylor. Indeed, Chapter 6 of Small is Beautiful (Schumacher 1974, p. 64) is titled 'The Greatest Resource – Education'. Monbiot (2000) warns us of the increasing commodification of education and the use of corporate-funded education packs to distort reality and mislead learners but, as Hutton (1995) had already argued, these and other posited dangers will only become irreversible problems if we stand back and allow them to happen. The purpose of a radical approach to citizenship education is to avoid such passivity.

Creating the future

If there is no point in predicting the future, we can at least plan for the future we would like, and work towards its accomplishment. Even better, we can work with our pupils to help them to imagine and then create the future they would want to live in. For some this might hint at social engineering; my intention has not been to hint but to be open and assertive. Wherever we place ourselves in the social structure or social order, it must be clear that 'all educational practices are profoundly political in the sense that they are designed to produce one sort of human being or another' (Postman 1970, p. 86) and that 'All debate about education is fundamentally political because it concerns the ultimate questions of what sort of people and societies we are trying to create' (Harber 2009, p. 7). We either want to develop a society in which people can participate and in which they wish to do so, or we do not. Those who pay lip-service to notions of participation as both possible and welcome but oppose the development of citizenship education and the changes it can bring about are equally guilty of social engineering – the difference between us is that they are opposed to change, opposed to participation, opposed to informed citizenry, opposed to progress.

We know that the gloomy perception that 'increasing numbers of children are arriving at early schooling showing symptoms of anxiety, emotional insecurity and aggressive behaviour. They seem devoid of many skills and suffer low self-esteem' (Arthur 2003, p. 3) is borne out by other studies. It is a waste of talent and of humanity as well as a source of social discord that such a situation exists, but we need to remember that it is not a universal condition, that there are also children who are well-balanced, secure in themselves, amenable in conduct, skilled and confident. Education is not the problem, but it could provide the answer . . . or, more accurately, it is that part of a much greater problem which might just enable people to find an answer which won't rend the social fabric beyond repair. Teachers have a fundamentally important role in addressing and repairing this situation, irrespective of its cause(s); those teachers might ask 'why me?' to which the unavoidable response must be 'why not? Look what happens when we leave it to someone else.'

In Case Study 1 at the conclusion of Chapter 2, the reader was enjoined to consider my reinterpretation of Postman and Weingartner's 16 principles of practice. Rudduck (1991) offers a much more concise list of the sort of demands the Humanities Curriculum Project (HCP) placed on participating teachers – '1. Discussion rather than instruction; 2. Teacher as a neutral chairperson; 3. Teacher talk reduced to about 15 per cent; 4. Teacher handling material from different disciplines; 5. New modes of assessment' (Ruddock 1991, p. 61) and she goes on to identify 'new skills for pupils' to acquire, 'new content for many classrooms' and 'organizational demands on schools'. While the HCP was not the new National Curriculum – in many ways it was more innovative and, by being restricted to one subject and for a fixed periods, less far-reaching – the demands and requirements Rudduck identified in relation to that project remain relevant in the wider picture. In the 15 years following Postman and Weingartner, some progress had been made to at least identifying and trying to effect some of the changes they recommended; a further 20 years have passed and there is still some way to go.

Postman and Weingartner (1976) suggest 11 strategies for teachers to understand their pupils and themselves. These strategies involve

1. questioning what the teacher has planned for pupils;
2. offer classes with questions and problems rather than answers;
3. do not allow contributions to discussion until the speaker can give a summary of the previous point which satisfies the person who made that point;
4. refuse to respond to any contribution which is not a question, offering a reward to the person who asks the most questions (NOT the 'best');
5. think about the information you do not have about a student which none the less influences the grade(s) you give her/him;
6. test the 'self-fulfilling prophecy' by believing your pupils are the smartest (possibly in their terms if not yours) and treat them accordingly;
7. tell everyone on your course that they will have an A grade come what may, then get them to plan the course content according to what they think they need to know;
8. teach to the future, not the past – concentrate on 'what if' rather than 'way back when';
9. remember that, no matter what you are teaching, media are important;
10. follow a series of questions which lead ultimately to – 'why do I teach?'

As with the educational Chartism mentioned in Chapter 2, some of this might already take place [e.g. 2 and 6 above would be seen as good practice, and not only within a citizenship education classroom] and some of it might still be regarded as utopian and unworkable [e.g. 4 and 7]. That doesn't mean it is not worth a try in order to address the final question. Day (2004) writes of passion for one's subject, for teaching, and for the future of young people as essential emotional characteristics for teachers. It may be that there are people who have drifted into teaching or while teaching who never had or no longer have such passions. Although 30 years have passed between Postman and Weingartner's work and that of Day, the message has not changed – if you do not care with a passion about your pupils and about your subject, if you think that you the teacher are the most important element of the educational process, then get out of teaching.

Despite the tone, this is not put forward as a criticism or attack. People get jaded. People's attitudes, interests, talents, preferences, passions can change. If a person is no longer committed to upholding the law, one would expect that they cease to be a police officer. If a person no longer cares about the health of others, one might commonly expect them to cease being a doctor. If a person is no longer committed to the principles of learning and personal development, goes this argument, one could reasonably expect them to recognize their new or previously submerged commitments, and give up teaching. If self-examination and reflection can help someone to that conclusion, it is a good thing. Day's expressed hope is that such reflexivity will reinvigorate teachers' reasons for entering the profession, and he recognizes that, for some, those reasons will have been lost forever rather than submerged or neglected. It might be that the caring and beliefs remain, but the will to see them through has been spent; the damage caused to pupils, and to the teacher, is pretty much the same – as is the plea to leave teaching to those who still can. (That there may be police officers and doctors who no longer care or cope does not devalue this line of argument, but suggests the strategy might be equally applicable to those and other occupations.)

What Postman and Weingartner wrote about 'the new education' almost 40 years ago could be applied to citizenship education today.

> It consists of having students use the concepts most appropriate to the world in which we all must live. All of these concepts constitute the dynamics of the question-questioning, meaning-making process that can be called 'learning how to learn'. . . The purpose is to help all students develop built-in, shockproof crap detectors as basic equipment in their survival kits. (Postman and Weingartner 1976, p. 204)

Reading

An often overlooked aspect of learning how to learn – at least at secondary level – is the continued development of reading. Teachers often value reading because it is so central to what we do, but can be reluctant to encourage or demand that their pupils read. As Draper (2001) observes, '[m]any kids today don't read much, and they don't read well. They learn to read in school, basically, but many times they don't learn to love reading in the process' (p. 12). We should be aware of the importance of the world which reading opens up, as when Foley (2010) cites research by the USA's National Endowment for the Arts (NEA) which concluded that 'readers are more likely than non-readers to take exercise, become actively involved in sport, go to museums, theatres, concerts, engage in voluntary work and vote in elections' (p. 141). While this might not be conclusive proof that reading makes one a good and active citizen, it certainly suggests that regular reading helps – particularly when we consider the notion of effective reading as literacy described by Blake et al. in their 'Chapter 6: Our most holy duty: Language and literacy' (p. 88).

If reading is a key to the development of citizens, then the use of language can be understood to be crucial. From the work of

Bernstein and Labov teachers have become familiar with the significance and power of school language, teacher language, as opposed to non-standard language. Language constitutes an essential element of cultural capital, it gives access not only to learning but to expression and persuasion. Illich discusses the phenomenon that '[s]chools operate under the slogan "education!" while ordinary language asks what children "learn".' (1973, p. 104), noting the shift from noun to verb, from a thing to an action, and he makes the rediscovery of language one of the three key elements for social recovery. I would add the rediscovery of other languages to be crucial; we cannot enable young people to become globally aware citizens – or even, increasingly, communicating citizens of their own locality – if they cannot speak with and understand the cultures and traditions of their neighbours. It is clear that learning languages other than English, and learning about the societies in which those languages are used, is vital to the development of citizenship education.

Not all cases are examples of excellence or merit replication. Unfortunately, some good ideas seem to get lost for bureaucratic reasons or personal preferences, of which Case Study 13 is one example.

Case study 13

One school which gives outstanding support to some of my PGCE Citizenship student teachers and an excellent citizenship education experience to its pupils had a policy until recently that every lesson in every non-practical subject began with pupils reading for ten minutes. This enabled the teacher to arrive unstressed, set up whatever activities need to be set up, engage with pupils who require individual attention (whether at their own behest or the teacher's), and ensure a clear start. It also enabled pupils to engage with the teacher, have time to reach classes unstressed, leave any hassles from previous lessons behind, spend some time following an interest, and to have a quiet and unpressured ten minutes every hour. It also, of course, developed reading skills – not only the ability to make sense of marks on a page, but to understand the information and arguments and to bring these to classroom-based activities when relevant – and the pleasure of reading.

Following a highly unfavourable Ofsted inspection, the school's senior management team decided to stop this practice. I was told that Ofsted did not approve of the practice yet, on scrutinizing the inspection report, the only reference I could find to it tells us that '[s]ensible steps are being taken to increase pupils' ability to access the curriculum. For instance, non-practical lessons begin with a short period of reading'. It is difficult to equate 'did not approve' with 'sensible', and one cannot help but conclude that, wilfully or otherwise, the report was either misunderstood or used to introduce a retrograde change while blaming a convenient bogey man. Undoubtedly neither the first nor last time that such a strategy has been employed, it is a great pity that such an effective approach to learning was jettisoned for no tangible benefit to anyone. More time for structured teaching does not necessarily equate with more effective learning.

Developing opportunities

Citizenship education is part of a pupil's entitlement; not for a few days a year, nor one hour a fortnight, nor hidden away in another subject, but at all times. Discrete subject provision, no matter how well presented, organized and delivered, cannot ensure this entitlement on its own, any more then numeracy or literacy or ethics can be the exclusive domain of specific subjects. There can be no doubt that

> [t]o sequester the responsibility for citizenship within a single discipline . . . or even a single class . . . is a grave mistake . . . students need multiple opportunities to develop skills and aptitudes that facilitate effective citizenship (Smith et al. 2010, p. 9)

and that schools have a responsibility to avoid that grave mistake. We need to plan for collaboration between teachers, not for them to look at ways in which they can pinch bits of the citizenship education curriculum for 'their' subject or claim that they are already providing citizenship education through what they do.

Teachers need to regard citizenship education as an opportunity rather than a threat. Not as an opportunity to enhance their subject, but one through which to enhance their pupils. If pupils care about their society and their futures, if they care about themselves and are empowered to initiate changes and face consequences, they are much more likely to engage with their peers and with their teachers. They will have reasons to learn rather than to be as anxious, insecure, and unskilled as Arthur (2003) found many of them to be. There are challenges to teaching citizenship just as there are in all subjects. A generation ago ICT was perceived by many teachers as a threat – it probably still is by some – as a new subject with a new language and with applications (in a traditional, non-ICT sense) beyond our understanding. Nobody would doubt the importance of young people being technologically literate, even if we would not all agree that the National Curriculum identifies the best way to achieve this. ICT is commonly an integral part of the teaching and learning which takes place in other subjects; it has not been annexed or subsumed, but harnessed with at least the intention of supporting learning. The same has to become true of citizenship education.

As well as working with other subjects, we can see the development of working across phases of education. Case Study 5 in Chapter 4 stems from work relating to early years teaching; Case Study 2 in Chapter 2 is of a primary school; other school-related case studies relate to secondary education. One of the texts I have regularly cited is Smith et al. (2010), a collection of essays discussing citizenship education in further and higher education in the USA. Citizenship barely starts at 16 in England in terms of opportunities for independent involvement, but compulsory citizenship education stops at that age. As Case Study 14 indicates, building on citizenship education in schools by making it a compulsory and intrinsic element of further and higher education could serve to enable young people to continue their development and therefore both shape and meet the needs of society.

Case study 14

A proposal for the introduction of global citizenship into the university curriculum of Nigeria (© Kola Adesina and Durotimi Adeboye Reproduced with permission.)

Kola Adesina, of the *Crescent University Abeokuta,* and Durotimi Adeboye, of Lagos Schools Online Project, aspire to introduce a coherent citizenship education curriculum throughout all stages of education in Nigeria – primary, secondary and tertiary. Kola's proposal for this to his university identifies a litany of alarms with which many readers will be familiar. They desire to challenge intolerance, exploitation and inequality, to disseminate the principles of democracy for Africa and show why corrupt practices should never be accepted. The examples they intend to use and the key problems they wish to address might be specifically Nigerian and more generally African, but there is a great deal that teachers, students and pupils in other countries and other continents can learn from their approach.

Arthur (2005, p. 4) suggests that, for a variety of reasons, 'one would expect universities to demonstrate a clear commitment to a culture of citizenship. This would include encouraging students to understand the importance of an active citizenry'. For those of us who hold such expectations, Adesina and Adeboye show one way forward.

A proposal for the introduction of global citizenship into the university curriculum of Nigeria

KOLA ADESINA Head of Department of Mass communication and coordinator of Global Citizenship Studies, *Crescent University Abeokuta*. His research interests include the mass media and Citizenship Studies.

Background

The intention is to contribute to the Nigerian educational system through the introduction of citizenship in schools. The need to promote citizenship in Nigeria's schools is of paramount importance to the survival of good governance, democracy, peace and unity in the country. The recent level of moral decadence in schools, juvenile delinquency, the spread of social miscreants, corruption, vandalism and terrorism are clear warnings of the dangers ahead if adequate measures are not taken to curb the situation.

Incessant religious riots, wanton destruction of public properties, disrespect for law and order, total disregard and disrespect of parents by their growing children

Case study 14 *Continued*

and lack of commitment to public service coupled with the get-rich-quick syndrome are common features of Nigerian society. This ugly situation is exacerbated by increasing level of poverty among the populace.

This proposal is a call to action for developing responsible citizens of this great Nation through education and empowerment with emphasis on youth development. It is an exercise meant to examine, in all its ramifications, the possibility of introducing citizenship studies into school curriculum in Nigeria from the Primary – Secondary – Tertiary level during the formative years of the youth with the ultimate aim of producing responsible citizens as a hope for future generations.

By incorporating and inculcating the principles of citizenship into education, it will enable young people to develop concerns for peaceful coexistence among one another, challenge poverty and injustice, and take real effective and decisive actions for change. Nigeria needs a change. Developing the potentials of youth is a great challenge.

Aims and objectives:

The main aim of the proposed project is to design a course to be taught as citizenship in Nigeria's primary, secondary and tertiary schools curricula. It is meant to bridge the gaps that exist between communities and groups in Nigeria as a result of practice, prejudice, myths, a combination of these and other factors.

The specific objectives are:

i. To teach citizenship as a subject at all levels from primary – secondary – tertiary education in Nigerian schools.

ii. To create awareness in Nigeria of the multiethnic, multicultural and multi-faith nature of most communities and the acceptance of these as a reality of the modern world we live in, as an antidote for ethnic and religious intolerance.

iii. To reduce or eliminate the chances of young people being exploited or used for destructive exercises because of their ignorance.

iv. To teach the principles of democracy as the best method of governance, how it is practised and abused in Africa.

v. To show corruption, in their various forms, as the bane of many African societies and why corrupt practices should never be accepted as normal.

vi. To teach and emphasize the removal of barriers between communities in Africa, emphasizing the damaging effects of violence and conflicts and their role in perpetuating poverty in Africa, using graphic illustrations of genocides in places like Rwanda and Sierra Leone.

vii. Highlighting the deprivation and exploitation of women with emphasis on how such contribute to promoting perpetual poverty in Africa.

viii. To adapt aspects of the Millennium Development Goals (MDGs) including the effect of HIV/AIDS and other health issues.

ix. To teach peace and conflict resolution at both secondary and tertiary education in Nigerian schools in order to develop mediation skills in young people.

x. To create awareness of the unacceptable growing levels of poverty in Nigeria and how at individual level preventive and reversal actions can be taken.

Methodology:

The strategy is to reorient minds by targeting the youth through education and empowerment.

To achieve the set objectives, the working committee initiated will design a course that will be a part of a wider subject – Citizenship.

This will be set at various key stages and will be a compulsory subject in the primary and secondary school curriculum most especially. Its contents will be developed in consultation with organizations responsible for curriculum development in Nigeria.

Global Citizenship studies will assist government in finding ways of developing the potential of the Nigerian Youth in order for them to be better able to face the leadership challenges of the future. As children mature citizenship education will contribute positively to their mental and physical development. This contribution will ensure a solid foundation for the country's future.

The following synopsis is premised on the Nigerian situation with special focus on cultural values and attendant crises arising from finding a positive place for the country in the global village. It has been structured with view to adapting it across the developing world.

1. Morals, values and attitude development

Concepts of time and punctuality; Respect for elders and constitutes authority; Concern for the environment; Empathy and commitment to common good; Self-esteem and sense of identity; Charitable and humanitarian services.

2. Knowledge and understanding

Social justice and equity; Global interdependence; Sustainable development; Heritage studies.

3. Skills development

Critical thinking and analysis; Arguing effectively; Challenging injustice and inequalities; Showing respect for people and things; Cooperation and conflict prevention; Legal enterprise and legitimate wealth creation.

⇨

Case study 14 *Continued*

Endnote

This would appear to be a significant challenge for a country where most education is provided by private concerns rather than state authorities, with the world's eighth largest population (almost 150 million), 250 ethnic groups, 68 per cent literacy and 70 per cent of the workforce engaged in agriculture. Kola Adesina and Durotimi Adeboye argue that these are reasons why this project is imperative, and I have to wonder why many wealthier and more literate countries are not following Nigeria's example in striving to develop a coherent citizenship programme throughout all stages of education.

Summary

There are further topics to be discussed which this book has not explicitly addressed. While matters of school ethos and the development of teacher skills and confidence must be addressed if citizenship education is to continue to be more than just another subject, the other aspects of citizenship education considered here do not constitute an exhaustive list. Awareness and celebration of identity and diversity, the development of personal voice and the ability to have it heard, the will and ability to become politically engaged, understanding how to be an effective and active citizen, the ability to assess and influence social order – all of these are attributes essential to citizens and for society. But they are not all that is required; we need, for example, citizens who can conduct themselves rationally and autonomously. There may be other categories, other skills, other attributes which underpin being a citizen in and of the twenty-first century. These will only be established though discussion and achieved through insight, engagement and application, and I look forward to the insights, arguments and recommendations of others which will support the development of a radical approach to all of citizenship education.

Not only does more have to happen in schools – not so much more content as more opportunity, more learning rather than more teaching – but we have to look beyond compulsory education.

The final words, for the moment, must go to someone who has done more to shape many young people's worlds than any educator of the last 15 years. For all the pressure on children to read more (or at all) which came from carers, teachers, politicians, librarians and others, it was a series of books set in a world of everyday magic which achieved what so many of those of us who might deem ourselves experts tried so hard and for so long to achieve. If we want young people to be able to grasp our damaged society and make it something worth celebrating, we need to give them the opportunity to do so. We should not be in any doubt that there are as many capable, interested, articulate, creative and imaginative young people now as in the days of our own youth, just as there are probably as many disenchanted, disinclined and despondent youngsters now as then. If young people are to make the most of who they are and what they offer, they have to be properly informed and equipped to make the decisions that matter. To paraphrase Albus Dumbledore, the headmaster of Hogworts, our strengths lie not in our talents but in our choices (Rowling 1998).

Glossary

Most of the language in this book should be accessible to the majority of readers. I am aware that some terms used are nationally or even regionally specific, and that many are contentious. What follows is not necessarily an exhaustive list of such terms, nor do I claim absolute accord with any reputable dictionary; they are the terms I think need to be clarified, and the clarifications relate to my use of them. By the time this book is published it is likely that some of the terms will have become obsolete, particularly those which relate to governmental administration, policy and bureaucracy – this is one of the perennial challenges of the world of education and not unique to the United Kingdom.

ASBO – Anti-Social Behaviour Order

A penalty imposed by courts in England to limit where and with whom a person can meet, issued in response to behaviour considered to be threatening or damaging to a public sense of comfort or safety. These are popularly perceived to be aimed at young people, although they are not always the recipients of such orders, and there is a further popular perception that the young upon whom such orders are imposed regard them as badges of honour rather than penalties or punishments.

Beginning Teacher
Sometimes offered as a synonym for student teacher and one which, like trainee teacher, indicates a philosophical position relating to the development of teachers. Some student teachers are far from beginners, having worked as unqualified teachers or instructors, teaching assistants, as teachers of English as a foreign or second language; this term implies to me a disregard for any previously developed skills or experience. (*see Student, Trainee*)

Citizenship Education
The preferred term in this book, used to make clear the difference between the National Curriculum subject of Citizenship, the condition of being a citizen, and the processes and tests through which people go in order to be granted that condition.

CPD – Continuing Professional Development
A collective term for the training provided for teachers to enable them to keep up to date with developments in their subjects and in education more generally. This usually takes place in school on days when pupils are not attending, or in 'twilight sessions' after school, or at weekends.

DCFS – Department for Children, Families and Schools, renamed after the 2010 General Election as the Department for Education (DfE).
The government department responsible for most aspects of education in England.

England
The most populous region of the United Kingdom, often misused as a synonym for the UK or for Britain – particularly in the mass media and, for reasons I cannot fathom, by reputable and otherwise scrupulously careful historians. The four component parts of the United Kingdom (Scotland, Wales, Northern Ireland

and England) have separate education systems; the National Curriculum is not national at all as it applies only to England.

GSCE – The General Certificate in Secondary Education

A series of examinations and other forms of assessment undertaken by pupils, usually but not always at the end of Year 11 – at or approaching 16 years of age.

ICT – Information and communications technology

One of the compulsory subjects within the National Curriculum for England and one which, like Citizenship Education and Religious Education, is often taught by non-specialists and not always in accordance with either statutory requirements or advisory guidelines.

ITE – Initial teacher education

Sometimes seen as a synonym for ITT, but there is a philosophical difference (see ITT, beginning teacher, student, trainee).

ITT – Initial teacher training

Sometimes seen as a synonym for ITE, but there is a philosophical difference (see ITE, beginning teacher, student, trainee).

KS – Key Stage

Education in England is divided into age bands, known as key stages (KS): KS 1 (5–8 year olds) and KS2 (8–11) mark the primary phase, KS 3 (11–14), KS 4 (14–16) are secondary. The 16–18 age band is often referred to as KS 5, but it is not as it is not an element of compulsory education and therefore not a Key Stage. Secondary schools are increasingly truncating KS3 to allow more time for a variety of activities, including early preparation for public examinations, so that there is a move away from the original age categories.

Master's Level

Student and other teachers have opportunities to submit work which can contribute towards the award of higher level academic credits, 180 of which can result in the achievement of a Master's degree – increasingly in Teaching and Learning (MTL).

National Curriculum

Established in 1988, updated and restructured several times, this indicates/dictates the teaching and learning required to take place in state schools. Citizenship Education was originally a cross-curricular theme but, since 2002, it has been a compulsory subject in Key Stage 3 and 4. Strictly speaking (see England above, and Bailey (1996)) it is not national at all.

NQT – Newly Qualified Teacher

Having gained a PGCE, teachers who embark upon their first year in a teaching post continue to be given structured support and development (CPD). The NQT year must be successfully completed in order for a teacher to be regarded as fully qualified.

Ofsted – the Office for Standards in Education

A qango with responsibility for monitoring and reporting upon standards of teaching and learning in schools and in initial teacher education and training. Such has been the improvement in its relationship with schools that an impending Oftsed inspection in now only regarded with dismay rather than, as formerly, outright terror.

PGCE – Postgraduate Certificate in Education/Professional Graduate Certificate in Education

One of the teaching qualifications available for those with degrees and who wish to teach. The initials stand for either Postgraduate Certificate in Education or Professional Graduate Certificate in Education, dependent on the level of credits achieved.

Pupil – Young learner

This term is preferred here to differentiate such learners from those who are studying how to teach them and is used throughout unless cited authors use the term 'student'. In such cases the context of the quotation should make the meaning clear.

QCA – Qualifications and Curriculum Agency

A qango which was renamed Qualifications and Curriculum Development Agency and which ceased to exist shortly after the Conservative/Liberal Democrat government took office in May 2010.

Radical

To promote, embrace and reflect ideas and actions which are significantly different from current and past practice.

Student – Someone who is studying to become a teacher

As well as separating such people from the younger learners referred to here as pupils, the term also reflects a philosophical position regarding the development of teachers. It is a principle of radical education that teaching is not about applying set processes to specific circumstances and understanding the mechanics of instruction, but that it involves study, reflexivity, development and questioning. (See Beginning Teacher, Trainee)

Subnational

Possibly a neologism used to try to differentiate between those regions of the United Kingdom which have some historical claims to be separate nations but which are now constituent parts of a whole. These parts are not politically equal as Scotland has a parliament while Wales has an assembly and Northern Ireland has a different type of assembly and England has none of these, although some would claim that the parliament which sits in Westminster is largely English in make-up and focus. The status of The Isle of Man, Cornwall, The Kingdom of Fife or other regions with some sense of separate identity is not implied or considered in my usage.

Subversive

As used by Postman and Weingartner (1976), facing up to and attempting to resolve social problems while consciously undermining the attitudes and processes which produce them.

Trainee

A term used by those who consider teaching to be about applying set processes to specific circumstances and understanding the mechanics of instruction, rather than involving study, reflexivity, development and questioning. The term often used by governmental and teacher qualifying bodies and adopted by others without necessarily considering the implications of the term. (See Beginning Teacher, Student)

Volunteer

When used as a noun this should indicate someone who has freely chosen to participate in an activity, usually unpaid. If used as a verb it is the action of choosing to so participate. This term is often used in relation to citizenship education as a wholly inaccurate euphemism for persuaded, coerced or compelled, as when pupils are given no choice but to participate in an activity; if pressure is brought to bear, the pressured person is not a volunteer and the activity is therefore not voluntary.

Weltanshuuang

A Weberian term approximating to 'world view' but perhaps a little closer to 'the sense we make of the world around us as demonstrated by our actions and priorities'.

Bibliography

Books and Articles

Advisory Group on Citizenship (1998) *Education for Citizenship and the teaching of Democracy in Schools: Final Report of the Advisory Group on Citizenship*. London: QCA.

Ajegbo, K., Kiwan, D. and Sharma, S. (2007) *Curriculum Review – Diversity and Citizenship*. Nottingham: DfES.

Alderson, P. (2004) 'Democracy in Schools: Myths, Mirages and Making it Happen', in B. Linsley and E. Rayment (eds), *Beyond the classroom: Exploring active citizenship in 11–16 education*. London: New Politics Network, pp. 31–38

Apple, M. W. (1990) *Ideology and Curriculum*. London: Routledge.

Aronowitz, S. and Giroux, H. A. (1985) *Education under Siege: The Conservative, Liberal and Radical Debate Over Schooling*. London: Routledge and Kegan Paul.

Arthur, J. (2003) *Education with Character: The Moral Economy of Schooling*. London: RoutledgeFarmer.

—— (2005) 'Introduction', in J. Arthur with K. E. Bohlin (eds), *Citizenship and Higher Education: The Role of Universities in Communities and Society*. Abingdon: RoutledgeFalmer, pp. 1–7.

Arthur, J. and Wright, D. (2001) *Teaching Citizenship in the Secondary School*. London: David Fulton.

Bailey, R. (1996) 'The Irony of The National Curriculum', in D. Hayes, (ed.), *Debating Education: Issues for the new millennium?* Canterbury: Canterbury Christ Church College, pp. 14–18.

Baldelli, G. (1971) *Social Anarchism*. Middlesex: Penguin.

Bell, D. (2005a) 'Speech to the Hansard Society'. Available at: http://www.ofsted.gov.uk/ [accessed 1 October 2006].

—— (2005b) 'Education for Democratic Citizenship – The Roscoe Lecture at Liverpool John Moores University'. Available at: http://www.ofsted.gov.uk/ [accessed 11 December 2006].

Berg, L. (1972) *Risinghill: Death of a Comprehensive*. Harmondsworth: Penguin.

Bernstein, B. (1973) *Class, Codes and Control Vol 1: Theoretical Studies towards a Sociology of Language*. London: Paladin.

Bernstein, J. L. (2010) 'Citizenship-Oriented Approaches to the American Government Course', in M. B. Smith, R. S. Nowacek and J. L. Bernstein (eds), *Citizenship across the Curriculum*. Bloomington: Indiana University Press, pp. 13–35.

Best, G. and Scott, L. (1994) *The Best of Times*. London: Simon and Schuster.

Blake, N., Smeyers, P., Smith, R. and Standish, P. (2000) *Education in an Age of Nihilism*. London: RoutledgeFalmer.

Bowles S. and Gintis H. (1976) *Schooling in Capitalist America*. London: Routledge & Kegan Paul.

Breslin, T. (2005) 'Delivering National Curriculum Citizenship: Comparing and Applying Curriculum Models', in T. Breslin and B. Dufour (eds), *Developing Citizens*. London: Hodder Murray, pp. 309–19.

Brett, P. (2004) ' "More Than a Subject": Fair Play for Citizenship'. Available at: http://www.citized.info/index.php?strand=2&r_menu=res [accessed 1 October 2005].

—— 'Identity and Diversity: Citizenship Education and looking forward from the Ajegbo Report'. Available at: http://www.citized.info/?strand=0&r_menu=res [accessed 30 June 2008].

Brown, N. and Fairbrass, S. (2009) *The Citizenship Teacher's Handbook*. London: Continuum.

CCCS Mugging Group (1975) 'Some Notes on the Relationship between the Societal Control Culture and the News Media', in S. Hall and T. Jefferson (eds), *Resistance through Rituals*. London: Hutchinson, pp. 75–79.

Centre for Studies on Inclusion in Education (CSIE) (2000) *Index for Inclusion: Developing Learning and Participation in Schools*. Bristol: CSIE with CEN and CER.

Clay, J. and George, R. (2002) 'Equality and Inclusion', in V. Ellis (ed.), *Achieving QTS: Learning and Teaching in Secondary Schools*, Second Edition. Learning Matters: Exeter, pp. 138–51.

Cleaver, E., Ireland, E. and Kerr, D., (2003) 'The Citizenship Education Longitudinal Study', *Teaching Citizenship* Issue 7, 15–19.

Clemitshaw, G. (2008) 'A Response to Ralph Leighton's Article – "Revisiting Postman and Weingartner's 'New Education' – Is Teaching Citizenship a Subversive Activity?"' *Citizenship Teaching and Learning* 4 (1), 82–95.

Cohen, S. (ed.) (1994) *Folk Devils and Moral Panics: the Creation of the Mods and Rockers*. Oxford: Blackwell.

—— (1971) *Images of Deviance*. Harmondsworth: Penguin.

Cole, M. (ed.) (2000) *Education, Equality and Human Rights.* London: RoutledgeFalmer.

Corrigan, P. (1979) *Schooling the Smash Street Kids.* London: Macmillan.

Crick, B. (2004) 'Why Citizenship At All?' in B. Linsley and E. Rayment (eds), *Beyond the classroom: Exploring active citizenship in 11 – 16 education.* London: New Politics Network, pp. 5–10.

Davison, J. and Arthur, J. (2003) 'Active Citizenship and the Development of Social Literacy: A Case for Experiential Learning'. Available at: www.citized.info/pdf/commarticles/Arthur_Davison.pdf [accessed 10 March 2010].

Day, C. (2004) *A Passion for Teaching.* London: RoutledgeFalmer.

Dixon, B. (1979) *Catching Them Young 1.* London: Pluto Press.

Draper, S. M. (2001) *Not Quite Burned Out But Crispy Around the Edges.* Portsmouth, NH: Heinemann.

English Secondary Students Association (2009) Home Page. Available at: http://www.studentvoice.co.uk/ [accessed 5 November 2009].

Faulks, K. (2006a) 'Education for Citizenship in England's Secondary Schools: A Critique of Current Principle and Practice', *Journal of Education Policy* 21 (1), 59–74.

—— (2006b) 'Rethinking Citizenship Education in England', *Education, Citizenship and Social Justice* 1(2), 123–40.

Florio-Ruane, S. (2001) *Teacher Education and the Cultural Imagination: Autobiography, Conversation, and Narrative.* London: Lawrence Erlbaum.

Foley, M. (2010) *The Age of Absurdity: Why Modern Life Makes it Hard to be Happy.* London: Simon and Schuster.

Freeman, M. (1995) 'Children's Rights in a Land of Rites', in B. Franklin (ed.), *The Handbook of Children's Rights.* London: RoutledgeFalmer.

Geelan, D. (2010) 'Science, Technology and Understanding: Teaching the Teachers of the Citizens of the Future', in M. B. Smith, R. S. Nowacek and J. L. Bernstein (eds), *Citizenship Across the Curriculum.* Bloomington: Indiana University Press, pp. 147–64.

Gillborn, D (2006) 'Citizenship Education as Placebo: "Standards", Institutional Racism and Education Policy', *Education, Citizenship and Social Justice* 1 (1), 83–104.

Gillborn, D. and Mirza H. S. (2000) *Educational Inequality: Mapping Race, Class and Gender.* London: Ofsted.

Gipps, C. and Murphy, P. (1994) *A Fair Test? Assessment, Achievement and Equity.* Milton Keynes: Open University Press.

Giroux, H., (2000) 'Postmodern Education and Disposable Youth', in P. P. Trifonas (ed.), *Revolutionary Pedagogies: Cultural Politics, Instituting Education, and the Discourse of Theory.* London: RoutledgeFarmer, pp. 174–90.

Godwin, W. (1797) 'Education through Desire', in G. Woodcock, (ed.) (1980), *The Anarchist Reader.* Glasgow: Fontana/Collins, pp. 270–73.

Goffman, E. (1961) *Asylums*. Harmondsworth: Penguin.

Goodman, P. (1975) *Compulsory Miseducation*. London: Penguin.

Griffiths, M. (1998) *Educational Research for Social Justice: Getting off the Fence*. Buckingham: Open University Press.

Halualani, R. T. (2010) 'De-Stabilizing Culture and Citizenship: Crafting a Critical Intercultural Engagement for University Students on a Diversity Course', in M. B. Smith, R. S. Nowecek and J. L. Bernstein (eds), *Citizenship Across the Curriculum*. Bloomington: Indiana University Press, pp. 36–53.

Harber, C. (2009) *Toxic Schooling: How Schools Became Worse*. Nottingham: Educational Heretics Press.

Hargreaves, D. H. (1967) *Social Relations in a Secondary School*. London: Routledge and Kegan Paul.

—— (2004) *Learning for Life: The Foundations Of Lifelong Learning*. Bristol: Polity Press.

Hayes, B., McAllister, A. and Dowds, L. (2006) 'In Search of the Middle Ground: Integrated Education and Northern Ireland', *Politics Research Update (no 42)* Access Research Knowledge: Northern Ireland. Available at: http://www.ark.ac.uk/publications/updates/update42.pdf [accessed 24 Feb 2010].

Henn, M., Weinstein, M. and Forrest, S. (2005) 'Uninterested Youth? Young People's Attitudes towards Party Politics in Britain', *Political studies* 53 (3), 556–78.

Hutton, W. (1995) *The State We're In*. London: Jonathan Cape.

Illich I. (1973) *Deschooling Society*. Middlesex: Penguin.

Jackson, B. and Marsden, D. (1970) *Education and the Working Class*. London: Penguin.

Kerr, D., Lopes, J., Nelson, J., White, K., Cleaver, E., Benton, T. (2007) *VISION versus PRAGMATISM: Citizenship in the Secondary School Curriculum in England. The Citizenship education Longitudinal Study: Fifth Annual Report*. London: NfER.

Kimberlee, R. H. (2002) 'Why Don't British Young People Vote?' *Journal of Youth Studies* 5 (1), 85–98.

Knott, S. (2007) 'Britishness'. http://citized.info/

Kolb, D. (1984) *Experiential Learning*. New Jersey: Prentice Hall.

Kynaston, D. (2008) *Austerity Britain 1945–51*. London: Bloomsbury.

Labov, W. (1969) 'The Logic of Non-Standard English', in N. Keddie (ed.) *Tinker, Tailor… The Myth of Cultural Deprivation*. Harmondsworth: Penguin, pp. 21–66.

Lawton, D. (1975) Class, Culture and the Curriculum. London: Routledge & Kegan Paul.

Lehman, S. (1999) *The Tibetans: A Struggle to Survive*. London: Virgin.

Leighton, R. (2002) 'Who Are you? A Discussion on Citizenship Provision'. Paper presented at the British Sociological Association conference, Leicester University, March 2002.

—— (2004a) 'What You Give Is What You Get: A Preliminary Examination of the Influence of Teacher Perceptions of the Role of Citizenship Education'. Available at: http://www.citized.info/ [accessed 10 March 2010].

—— (2004b) 'Fair Conflict Resolution Starts Here.' *Teaching Citizenship Issue 11, Summer 2004*, 26–31.

—— (2004c) 'The Nature of Citizenship Education Provision: An Initial Study.' *The Curriculum Journal* 15 (2), 167–84.

—— (2006) 'Revisiting Postman and Weingartner's 'New Education' – Is Teaching Citizenship a Subversive Activity?' *Citizenship and Teacher Education* 2 (1), 89–97.

—— (2010a) 'Active Citizenship', in L. Gearon (ed.), *Learning to Teach Citizenship in the Secondary School*, 2nd Edition. London: Routledge, pp. 135–43.

—— (2010b) 'The (F)utility of Focus Days in Developing Citizenship Education'. Paper presented at the International Citizenship Education Conference, St Andrew's University, July 2010.

Lockyer. A. (2003) 'Introduction and Review', in A. Locker, B. Crick and J. Annette (eds) *Education for Democratic Citizenship: Issues of Theory and Practice*. Aldershot: Ashgate, pp. 1–14.

Lorimer, D. (ed.) (2008) *Learning for Life: From Inspiration to Aspiration*. Dundee: Learning for life.

Lukes, S. (1974) *Power: A Radical View*. London: Macmillan.

Mahony, P. and Hextall, I. (2000) *Reconstructing Teaching*. London: Routledge/Farmer.

Manzoor, S. (2010) 'My Month of Being Jewish', *Guardian* (G2), 8 April 2010.

McEwen, A. (1999) *Public Policy in a Divided Society – Schooling, Culture and Identity in Northern Ireland*. Aldershot: Ashgate.

McGlynn, C. (2004) 'Education for Peace in Integrated Schools: A Priority for Northern Ireland?' *Child Care in Practice* 10 (2), pp. 85–94.

Merton, R. K. (1968) *Social Theory and Social Structure*. New York: Free Press.

Michels, R. (1949) *Political Parties*. Glencoe: Free Press.

Mills, C. W. (1980) *The Sociological Imagination*. London: Penguin.

Monbiot, G. (2000) *Captive State*. London: Pan.

Morgan, C. and Morris, G. (1999) *Good Teaching and Learning: Pupils and Teachers Speak*. Buckingham: Open University Press.

Morrall, C. (2010) *The Man Who Disappeared*. London: Sceptre.

Oakeshott, M. (1962) *Rationalism in Politics and Other Essays*. London: Methuen.

O'Connor, S. (2010) 'Why Am I Allowed to Work and Marry but Not Vote?' *Folkestone and Hythe Kentish Gazette*, 30 August 2010, p. 3.

Office for Standards in Education (2003) *Inspecting Citizenship 11–16*. London: HMSO.

—— (2006) *Towards Consensus? Citizenship in Secondary Schools*. London: HMSO.

—— (2009) Denbigh School Inspection Report. Available at: http://www.ofsted.gov.uk/oxedu_reports/display/(id)/109116 [accessed 1 June 2010].

—— (2010) *Citizenship Established?* Manchester: Ofsted.

Park, R. (1950) *Race and Culture*. New York: Free Press.

Peters, M. A. and Bulut, E. (2010) 'Education and Culture', in J. Arthur and I. Davies (eds), *The Routledge Educational Studies Textbook*. London: Routledge.

Peterson, A. and Knowles, C. (2007) 'PGCE Citizenship Student Teacher Understandings of Active Citizenship'. Available at: www.citized.info/pdf/com-marticles/ActiveProject-Report.pdf [accessed 15 January 2009].

Postman, N. and Weingartner, C. (1976) *Teaching as a Subversive Activity*. London: Penguin.

Postman, V. (1970) 'The Politics of Reading', in N. Keddie (ed.), *Tinker, Tailor . . . the Myth of Cultural Deprivation*. London: Penguin.

Powell, M. and Solity, J. (1990) *Teachers in Control: Cracking the Code*. London: Routledge.

Preston, J. and Chakrabarty, N. (2010) 'Do Schools Contribute to Social and Community Cohesion?' in J. Arthur and I. Davies (eds), *The Routledge Educational Studies Textbook*. London: Routledge, pp. 187–94.

Price, G. A. (2002) 'Inclusion: Special Educational Needs', in V. Ellis (ed.), *Achieving QTS: Learning and Teaching in Secondary Schools*. Exeter: Learning Matters..

Qualifications and Curriculum Authority (2007) *The National Curriculum for England*. Nottingham: QCA.

Rattray Taylor, G. (1974) *Rethink*. Middlesex: Penguin.

—— (1977) *How to Avoid the Future*. London: NEL.

Reid, A., Gill, J. and Sears, A. (2010) 'The Forming of Citizens in a Globalized World'. in A. Reid, J. Gill and A. Sears (eds), *Globalization, The Nation State and the Citizen: Dilemmas and Directions for Civics and Citizenship Education*. London: Routledge, pp. 3–16.

Riley, K. (2010) London Lives Student Voice Conference report. Available at: http://www.leru.org.uk/london_lives Accessed 3 July 2010.

Ross, A. and Dooly, M. (2010) 'Young People's Intentions about Their Political Activity', *Citizenship Teaching and Learning* 6 (2), 43–60.

Rowling, J. K. (1998) *Harry Potter and the Chamber of Secrets*. London: Bloomsbury.

Rudduck, J. (1991) *Innovation and Change*. Buckingham: Open University Press.

Schumacher, E. F. (1974) *Small is Beautiful; a Study of Economics As If People Mattered*. London: Abacus.

Sellar, W. C. and Yeatman R. J. (1976) *And Now All This*. London: Magnum.

Smith, J. A. and Osborn, M. (2003) 'Interpretative Phenomenological Analysis', in J. A. Smith (ed.), *Qualitative Psychology*. London: Sage, pp. 53–80.

Smith, M. B., Nowacek, R. S. and Berstein, J. L. (2010) 'Introduction: Ending the Solitude of Citizenship Education', in M. B. Smith, R. S. Nowacek and J. L. Bernstein (eds), *Citizenship Across the Curriculum*. Bloomington: Indiana University Press, pp. 1–12.

Thomas, W. I. and Thomas, D. (1928) *The Child in America: Behavior Problems and Programs*. New York: Knopf.

Toffler, A. (1973) *Future Shock*. London: Pan.

Weber, M. (2009) *From Max Weber: Essays in Sociology*. London: Routledge.

Werder, C. (2010) 'Fostering Self-Authorship for Citizenship: Telling Metaphors in Dialogue', in M. B. Smith, R. S. Nowacek and J. L. Bernstein (eds), *Citizenship Across the Curriculum*. Bloomington: Indiana University Press, pp. 54–72.

White, R. with Brockington, D (1983) *Tales Out of School: Consumers' views of British Education*. London: Routledge & Kegan Paul.

Wilde, O. (1891) 'Disobedience: Man's Original Virtue', in Woodcock, G. (ed.) (1980), *The Anarchist Reader*. Glasgow: Fontana/Collins, pp. 72–74.

Williams R. (2010) 'Union Says Pupils on Interview Panels are Humiliating to Teachers'. *Guardian* Newspaper 3/4/2010.

Willis, P. (1977) *Learning to Labour*. Farnborough: Saxon Press.

Young, J. (1971) *The Drugtakers: the Social Meaning of Drug-taking*. London: Paladin.

Websites

http://www.ark.ac.uk – Research on Northern Ireland.

http://www.citized.info/ – The URL for citizenship education in the UK (now archived).

http://www.debatingmatters.com/ – Guide to information about a debating completion which emphasizes how to marshal knowledge and decide what is relevant and when.

http://www.denbigh.net/ – Denbigh School, Milton Keynes.

http://www.environment.gov.au/education/aussi/ – The Australian Sustainable Schools Initiative supports schools and their communities to develop inclusive and holistic approaches to sustainability.

http://www.leru.org.uk/ – London Education Research Unit, a resource area for information about Education in London.

http://www.ofsted.gov.uk/ – The UK government agency for monitoring and inspecting schools.

http://www.persona-doll-training.org/ukhome.html – Information on how to purchase or borrow dolls and how to access training.

http://www.rumad.org.au/ '– Are You Making A Difference?' aims to encourage greater civic and social participation.

http://www.studentvoice.co.uk/ – The English Secondary Students Association, providing representation for pupils in England's secondary schools.

http://www.wedg.org.uk – The World Education Development Group, a Canterbury, UK, based organisation dedicated to raising awareness of diversity, identity and international cooperation.

Index

Frequently occurring themes such as 'citizenship education', 'national curriculum', 'pupils', 'questions', 'radical education' and 'young people', can be found throughout the text.